The Incompatibility of Men and Women

And How to Overcome It

The Incompatibility of Men and Women
And How to Overcome It

by Julius Fast

Published by M. Evans and Company, Inc., New York
AND DISTRIBUTED IN ASSOCIATION WITH
J. B. Lippincott Company, Philadelphia and New York

For Barbara—who taught me compatibility

Contents

Contents

1

The Perfect Match

If Men Played Cards as Women Do

When I was a youngster in an all-boys camp, a good many years ago, we had an amateur night once a week and each tent put on a brief skit or playlet. Our tent had a sure-fire winner guaranteed to bring the house down at least once each season. It was called "If Men Played Cards as Women Do."

The idea of the skit was that four men get together for a game of cards and act the way women act. They discuss each other's suits and hats. They are catty, gossipy and bitchy, and they drag out a quarter of an hour of small talk before the skit's climax, a summing up of the number of months between a friend's marriage and the delivery of his baby. The actors and the audience realize there are only six months as the lights black out.

I don't remember which the audience enjoyed more—the racy, for those days, denouement, or the spectacle of men acting the way women act. I think it was the latter, because the skit was recently dragged out of mothballs and produced on television with four big-name Hollywood actors. The final blackout was changed so that all four climbed on chairs and screamed at the sight of a mouse. Today an early pregnancy is neither funny nor daring.

I have wondered why men acting with all the weaknesses and tolerantly accepted foibles of women still make a funny spectacle. Why, in this time of changing values and roles and feminine liberation, are men still laughing at women?

I was visiting a psychiatrist friend one night last year when just such a skit came on TV. We both sat quietly watching the audience in the studio scream with laughter.

"What makes that skit so funny?" I asked my friend.

"Don't you see?" he replied. "That is their way of handling their frustration at their inability to cope with the opposite sex."

"Why can't they cope with the opposite sex? You're always telling me this is the age of psychological enlightenment."

"Because basically most men and most women are incompatible. We may know more about sexual mechanics and the inner psyche than ever before, but we're still very hung up on masculine and feminine ideals."

Just what are the guidelines of masculinity and femininity? What makes a man manly and a woman womanly? The easiest way to answer this question is to start with society's definition of a man and a woman. On the surface this seems a pretty stupid question. Surely if you take a man and a woman and strip them down there will be no question of what makes a man or what makes a woman. There are basic physical differences. But for many reasons the question goes deeper than these surface appearances. There are men who are masculine on the outside and yet feminine in deeper, more hidden ways. There are also masculine men who are completely homosexual. Are they any less masculine because they are homosexual or are they more masculine because they relate only to other men and completely reject the world of women? We are often told that more masculine men prefer the company of other men to that of women.

The same problems arise when we try to define womanliness. There are masculine women and feminine women. There are women who are only heterosexual and yet are aggressively masculine in all their dealings. Other women who are homosexual are extremely feminine, womanly, delicate—call it what you will.

The question is obviously not answered by simply investigating surface sexuality. We have to look beyond the shape to find the real inner man or woman.

The All-American Couple

Let's, for starters, take a close look at Joe. We all know Joe. He is the epitome of the American Male, masculine in all aspects of his life.

Joe is about thirty-five and he lives in the suburbs of a big city. He has a good job as a supervisor with a construction company. Physically he has a rugged good-looking face, not quite handsome and not quite ugly, but a little of both. More than anything, it's a strong face. Joe is well built and in good condition. He's about six feet tall, give or take an inch, broad-shouldered and lean.

Joe is married and has three children and a pretty wife. His idea of being a good father is managing the little league. There aren't many arguments in Joe's family, mainly because Joe is very clearly the man in the house. He handles the finances and makes the important decisions—where the family should go in the summer, what sort of car to buy, how the money should be budgeted and even, though neither he nor Ann, his wife, care to admit it, who the two of them will vote for. There's no problem about these decisions for Ann goes along with them. Why? "Well, Joe is my husband," she says. "And he's a man. There are some things men know more about than women."

Joe and Ann have friends in common, but Joe has some of his own friends as well. Every Tuesday is poker night with the boys, two of whom Ann doesn't really know and only sees when the game is at Joe's house. On these nights she prepares refreshments and then goes out with some of the girls.

Let's look at Joe a bit more closely. What is he like intellectually? Politically? Sexually?

Intellectually? Well, Joe isn't much of an intellectual. Oh, he reads the newspapers and some of the news magazines but, since school, Joe hasn't read more than one or two best sellers.

Politically Joe is an independent. He votes for the man he thinks will be best, and never mind the party. What Joe likes in a candidate is strength and honesty. "I don't care about these long-haired do-gooders. I want a man who can help the country, not weaken it."

And sexually? Joe has a full sex life; mostly with Ann. Joe is the one who initiates sex, and while Ann enjoys it she rarely asks for it. Joe has some sexual activity outside his marriage, but this is not too frequent and usually coincides with a business trip.

Joe has his typical likes and dislikes. He starts to read the paper with the sports pages, and he hasn't missed a Sunday afternoon football game on TV in the past five years. Joe likes poker with the boys and fooling around with his car motor on weekends. He likes to get off with some of the boys for hunting trips, and off by himself to fish. He dislikes any discussion with Ann about furnishing the home—"That's your department," and so it goes.

Joe is, in short, a typically "masculine" man, just as Ann is a typically "feminine" woman. Let's take a brief look at Ann. What is she like?

Ann is five years younger than Joe, and she recognizes the extra knowledge and maturity of those years, plus Joe's masculine strength. Ann is still slim and pretty, her blond hair darkening just a bit, her face still youthful, her figure still a 36-26-38.

Ann considers herself happily married. She gives in to Joe on all the larger decisions, but has learned to manipulate him. Ann has a lovely home and is very proud of it. She hasn't worked since her marriage and doesn't feel she should. Her job is the house and the children, and she does a good job of taking care of both. Ann spends most of her time cleaning and decorating and cooking and caring for Joe and the children.

Ann has also accepted taking a back seat to Joe. "Except of course when he's sick," she says. "Then he's a baby, just like the children. But I guess all men are."

Outside the home Ann has a circle of women friends, "the girls." Some of them are part of the couples she and Joe occasionally visit or entertain, but others are her own friends, some still single, whom she sees at afternoon bridge games or coffee klatsches, get-togethers she knows would never interest Joe.

Intellectually, Ann admits she isn't Joe's equal. Certainly he knows more about the world around them. "I can't even balance a checkbook properly, and Joe is always scolding me for messing our accounts up." Yet Ann is more apt to read the current books than Joe is. Politically Ann is usually confused by the issues and grateful that Joe can explain them. And sexually—well, Ann enjoys sex, but more in terms of Joe than herself. "Most of my enjoyment comes from making him happy. Sex is something I can give him."

Ann's likes and dislikes are different from Joe's. She starts the paper with the woman's page and the entertainment section. On Joe's night out with the boys, Ann and some of the girls will try to get baby sitters and attend one of the local concerts, or visit one of the art galleries.

On the evenings when they entertain friends, Ann looks forward to the girls getting together in one corner of the room to talk clothes, furnishings and babies, while Joe and the boys argue politics, business and sports.

Ann, in short, is a typical woman, a feminine woman.

Above all, Ann and Joe consider themselves completely compatible. "We just fit together," she shrugs. "Joe has all the qualities I lack, he's down to earth and dependable and I love all the things Joe just doesn't bother with, but we get along together. We fit together and satisfy each other's needs."

What's Wrong With the Picture

There it is—the perfectly "compatible" couple, the masculine man and the feminine woman. Joe, content to be the dominant husband and father, the leader in the marriage, stronger and more aggressive; and Ann, content to be the submissive one, the follower, the keeper of the home.

There is only one problem with Joe and Ann. They don't really satisfy each other's deepest needs. They are drowning in the myth of our time. Their real emotional selves are suffocating inside models created by hundreds of women's magazine stories, by novels and television serials and Hollywood movies of the thirties, forties and fifties.

American men and women have accepted these cultural ideal types and constantly attempt to live up to them. We know what a masculine man is—we've been told and shown often enough. He's Paul Newman and John Wayne and Sean Connery in the movies and, if we are men, we try to imitate them, if not consciously then in fantasy.

And women unfortunate enough to find homemaking a terrible bore, and alive enough to think that talk about the kids and cooking is deadly and limiting, may feel guilty about their inability to fit into the mold society has created for them.

Even were we to assume some basis in reality for these ideals of male and female, it would very quickly become apparent that they are mismatched. The James Bond fantasy simply does not include Mrs. Goodhousekeeping as the bedmate of 007. So, while Joe projects himself into the American masculine daydream, Ann wanders, lost on the road between Betty Crocker's kitchen and the pad of the sensuous woman.

Will the Real Joe and Ann Please Stand Up?

There are many Joes in the world, and there are many Anns. There are even Joes who are married to Anns. But there are more, far more, who are pretending to be Joe or Ann, who are trying desperately to pass for what society dictates a real man or real woman should be. They have been presented with a standard of masculinity or femininity all their lives, and they know they should live up to that standard. If they don't, they are a little unusual, a little peculiar. If they do conform to the ideal, they find themselves frustrated and unfulfilled. Many who are unable to answer the recurring question, "What do I really want?" secretly wonder if something is wrong with them.

For men, there is always the specter of homosexuality staring them in the face. Until very recently, when the Gay Liberation Front took its first stand, a homosexual was something to laugh at, to make fun of and to be grateful you were not. Now, of course, the entire scene is shifting and in some urban and intellectual circles the fear and shame of being homosexual has been stood on its head. A case in point is found in the book *Barnett Frumer Is an Unbloomed Flower*. Leaving a West Side party with someone he had taken to be a very good-looking young lady but who later turned out to be his old college roommate, Roland McGruder, Barnett is not surprised to hear Roland say, "I myself am so heterosexual it's fantastic, but if the ticket of admission to the avante garde is an occasional pair of high heels, I say pay it."

But this is a humorous exaggeration of New York's most "in" crowd, and while an occasional writer wished he had the homosexual experience—even as he wished he had the black experience or the Jewish experience so that he might write of it with understanding—the vast majority of American men are still terrified of any lapse of masculinity. This terror, incidentally, is one of the reasons most American men dislike touching other men, why American fathers will rarely kiss their sons and why any sign of weakness in a man is hidden and masked. It is, in fact, one of the big reasons we cling to the masculine ideal and try so hard to emulate it.

Women try just as hard to emulate the feminine ideal, though Women's Lib would deny furiously that it is worthy of that name. In this sense I use the word "ideal" as a standard, a model of the normal woman that society sets up. It is, we are told, the average woman, and, like a carrot in front of a donkey, the image beckons us toward the happy woman. Conform to this ideal, be a submissive woman, and you will find that elusive bluebird of happiness, smack in your own backyard.

Dr. J. Dudley Chapman in a recent (1967) book on the feminine mind and body says:

The woman learns . . . that aggression must be controlled, and this too is repressed and driven inward. This drive, she finds, brings rewards of acceptance and attention and it becomes a gratifying element in her life. This gratification makes inward direction and inhibition, or aggression, somewhat erotic in nature and enriches her affective, or inner, life. She finds great and wonderful sufferings in love—it readies her for the rigors of masculine love and the vicissitudes and sacrifices of motherhood.

There it is. The bluebird of happiness. If you can come out from under the bird droppings, you may ask yourself, How did it all happen?

One psychiatrist I have spoken to gave me a provocative statistic. He told me that most of his patients below the age of ten are boy-children. It is this man's opinion that the most well-meaning mother cannot understand her boy-child, and measures his behavior by a female standard. Already surrounded by women teachers at school, and unable to find emotional support from his father, where else can he turn but to the myth for his masculine identity?

And if putting women down builds his ego up, the vicious cycle begins.

2

From the Man's Corner:
How Do Men See Women?

The S.H.I.T.S. Club

"What we have here," my friend told me as we sat down at the card table, "is an exclusive men's club. We call it the S.H.I.T.S. Club."

It was one of those "nights out with the boys," and Sam had asked me over for an evening of poker. Sam's wife had gone off early, leaving a platter of sandwiches and a refrigerator full of beer.

I picked up my cards and asked the expected. "What does S.H.I.T.S. stand for?"

"Speak Hate In Tender Syllables," Sam said. "I'll take two cards."

"I don't get it."

"It's like this. The girls think we get together to play cards, and sure, we play cards, but what we really get together for is to sound off to each other about our wives."

"We get it all out," Bob added. "It's therapeutic and what they don't know won't hurt them."

"Which reminds me," Tom broke in, laying down his cards. "You wanna hear the crazy thing Mary did this weekend? You know how I feel about checkbooks. . . ."

The story had a point, and the men all chuckled. But stronger than the point of the story, I felt, was the hostility behind Tom's telling. He had barely finished before Bob picked up with a stupid stunt his wife had pulled the day before, locking the car keys into the car, "while the motor was still running, mind you."

Sam topped this with another and then Tom took off again. The evening wore on, the poker game not at all bad, the "speaking" bewildering in its stored-up venom and hostility. If these men really see their wives this way, I wondered, why in hell do they stay married?

But on the way home, Bob, who was walking me part way, drew a deep breath and said sheepishly, "Well, we sound like a bunch of bastards, I guess."

"Oh, no . . ." I started to protest automatically.

"Oh, yes—and maybe we are, but you know—this is really a joke, this club, but deep down it helps. It gives us a chance to ventilate these feelings all husbands have—to let off steam."

"And you call yourselves the S.H.I.T.S.?"

"Yeah—well, the name has a double significance, you know. We do feel a bit like shits about it. We are guilty."

Bob was right. The guilt that all men feel when they attack the women they love—and they do it constantly— is so much a part of their basic feelings toward women that it surfaces in all situations and at all times. It even surfaces during sex.

The Husband Who Won't Fight

When I was a young man I earned my extra money as foreman of a puppetry workshop. One of the things that never stopped fascinating me was how, once on the bridge, a performer became completely engrossed in his role. The puppet became his alter ego—another identity, often completely different from his own.

One afternoon, after a furious argument in the workshop, one of the girls involved took a girl puppet and a boy puppet, and, thinking she was alone in the shop, began manipulating both while assigning them the roles of the two arguers. Unnoticed, I watched, fascinated, as she followed the argument to the completion she had desired, then bagged the puppets away and went back to her workbench. She was much more comfortable and a happier worker for the rest of the afternoon.

I think a valuable therapeutic hint can be taken from this incident. Puppets are dolls, and therapists have long understood the value of doll play among troubled children as well as adults. Primitive people were aware of this. There are many anthropological reports of youngsters being taught sex through the use of dolls. We also can teach ourselves through the use of dolls. The doll is sufficiently removed from us to make such learning initially impersonal, and yet close enough to us to allow us to benefit and learn from their manipulations.

The doll games in this book are designed to take ad-

| 23

vantage of both this removal and closeness and to allow the reader to work out his problems without at first involving himself. Once the motivation behind the problem is understood, the doll can easily be related to the manipulator.

The first game is based on the lesson learned from the S.H.I.T.S. Club. The guilt that comes from these one-way criticisms can build up and eventually spoil the sexual act. The object of the game is to learn to accept your own hostility without guilt. Hostility, a natural by-product of incompatibility, need not be a pleasure-reducing component of your relationship.

The husband who resists arguing with his wife, who refuses to allow his hostility to surface because "it is undignified" or "it gets into deadends" or "it doesn't add up to anything," usually ends up allowing his wife to win the arguments. The truth is, he won't fight because he's afraid that winning would involve destroying his wife and he has not reached that point.

What he must learn is that he can fight without destroying his wife, that fighting, in fact, will strengthen the relationship between them. He must learn that exposing and facing the problem will make the problem solvable, not unsolvable.

Stand Up and Fight

Purpose: To help the man or woman who has difficulty working through an argument with someone of the opposite sex.

The object of this game is to teach the man how to win.

While the woman watches, the man takes the male doll* and calls it MAN. He then takes the female doll and calls it WOMAN. He places them side by side

* You will find the dolls on the last pages of this book.

24 |

imagining them to be in any setting where an argument might take place: kitchen, dining room or bedroom.

Round one: the man plays both roles. He carries on an argument between MAN and WOMAN.

Round two: The man keeps the male doll and continues to play the role of MAN. The woman takes the female doll and plays the role of WOMAN. The argument continues. MAN, however, must have the last word. No matter what the course of the argument, he must always conclude it.

(If it is the other way around, a woman who won't argue, the roles are simply reversed, with the woman having the last word.)

Talk to Me, Harold

But to get back to how men see women, let's take a look at Harold and Martha. They have a good marriage in terms of all the things that we think of as good, important and meaningful. They have a house in the suburbs, two cars, three color television sets and four handsome children. The only thing Harold and Martha haven't got is the ability to speak to each other. Sometimes they overcome this lack with a good deal of drinking, more often by watching two of the three color television sets. The children use the third. Frequently they get around the problem by visiting

| 25

friends or having friends over. In these gatherings, the women form one group on the couch and the men form another, usually in the kitchen, for some obscure reason. Then Harold comes alive and the talk sparkles.

After one of these social evenings, Martha, very thoughtful, asked Harold, "Why don't you ever talk to me the way you were talking to Bill tonight? I didn't think I'd ever get you away. What was it all about?"

"Huh?" Harold looked at her uncomprehendingly. "You really want to know? You're not putting me on?"

"Of course not. What was so fascinating?"

"Well, it's this tax business Bill has set up. He's got this fantastic gimmick of setting up two different companies with different stock options and . . ."

Ten minutes later Martha yawned heavily and said, "Harold—I'm so beat I'm going to pass out on my feet if I don't get some sleep."

"Oh—sure, baby. I'm sorry, let's go upstairs."

Martha didn't ask any more about Harold's private talks. She was just grateful he didn't talk to her. For Harold, it just confirmed what he already knew: "You can't talk to a woman about real things—even a woman you love. With a man it's different, easier."

The Ideal Woman

Harold and the poker gang knew this about women, not instinctively but from hard experience. There were men's worlds and women's worlds and, while they both shared simultaneous space, they were light years apart. This separation of men and women is not a matter of class. Harold, with his own business, is upper middle class and Sam and his poker gang are middle class, but Al is a working-class man.

Al works on a construction crew and puts in a rough day. He knocks off early, it's true, but he earns his pay and Al likes nothing better than to relax after work in front of the TV set with a cold beer—unless it's getting out of the house and down to the corner bar where the boys hang out.

"I don't drink much," Al shrugs. "Hell, I can't remember the last time I was drunk. But it's the company of the guys I like. They're a great bunch, so I nurse my three beers for the evening. The point is, I'm alive down there. Like on the construction gang. I'm alive there too. We horse around, kid each other or talk serious. You can't do that with chicks —you just can't. My wife—she's a great gal, but she's all tied up with the house and kids. That's her thing and I wouldn't have it any other way. Me, I like company."

And the company Al likes is the company of men. This, indeed, makes Al more masculine, makes him feel alive and manly. He's aware of this and aware of what makes his wife feel womanly. "The house and the kids. That makes any woman a woman."

Harold too says, "The house and the kids," and adds, "and a fur coat when we can afford it and perfume at sixty bucks an ounce and a cruise to Bermuda any time the temperature drops below 30."

Sam and Bob and Tom say, "No understanding, that's how women are. No sense of humor either. We told the girls about the S.H.I.T.S. one night, and we could hardly

| 27

stop laughing. Not a smile out of them. That's the difference."

I sat down with a friend recently, a personnel director
for a large company, who has had years of training in
analyzing the hidden motives behind people's actions and
talk, and I asked him what he thought made a woman
womanly.

"Basically," he said, "it's a softness, a gentleness, an ability
to yield."

"You're talking of ideals. Take the women you know,
the women you've worked with, talked with and slept with.
What are their most womanly characteristics?"

"I'd say the ability to make me feel like a man."

"You're still thinking in terms of ideals. Put it this way.
What are the basic characteristics of the women you know?"

There was a long pause, and then he nodded. "I see what
you mean. As a rule, women are too manipulative or de-
manding. What I really feel is that they challenge my manhood. They want to run things."

"Then isn't that womanliness?"

"No, not really. A woman should be soft and submissive."

"You would like her to be that way, but you seem to find
them rough and prickly. Are women soft and submissive?"

"Well, some of them must be!"

As we talked he became more restless, uneasy, and finally
he said, "Look, I just don't like going into this. It upsets
me. It makes me feel uneasy."

That same feeling of unease, a threatened feeling, was a
very common reaction of at least half of the men I questioned. Just analyzing womanliness or manliness upset them
and many skirted the real issue by presenting their dream
picture of woman. In all I questioned close to a thousand

men and women about womanliness and manliness. The older men in my sample, men in their late forties and fifties, when pressed, would admit that they saw a woman being womanly in terms of men. *When she is admired by men. During sex. When she's being screwed.*

A few saw women achieving real womanliness when she dominated men, when she manipulated them. They saw women as the enemy, the threat to their manhood, the classic castrator.

Those who saw her deferring to men also saw her resenting it. "Let's face it," a forty-nine-year-old man told me. "Her chief characteristic is her ability to sit on her ass— and get tired." "Mother love," another over-fifty said, "along with narrowness and pettiness." *Unpredictable, illogical, intuitive.*

The younger men, however, as a rule had a gentler view. Those in their thirties saw her as emotional, needing security and needing love. *Understanding. Gentle. Soft and tender. Emotionally changeable.*

But again much of this was idealized. This, it turned out on further probing, was the way they would like to see women. The way they actually see them, the characteristic that rings a bell, is not that pleasant. "They're concerned with clothes, with themselves, with how they look and how men react to them. It's a narcissism that spells woman. Like the old joke of the woman looking in the mirror and saying, 'Boo, you beautiful thing!'"

Another group, a sizeable one too, in their middle thirties see women as objects to be used. *A woman is a woman when she's being screwed. I'll tell you what makes a woman feel womanly—a good cock! Sex. That's the answer. If a woman has it, she's a woman. Without it, she's dried up.* This, incidentally, was a predominantly working-class group.

The younger group, those under thirty, the natives of this post-World War II planet, often saw womanliness as a part of humanness. *There's no difference, man. She feels like a human being, then she feels like a woman.*

Others in this age group agree with older men and cite sex as the determining factor. *A man admires her, she feels like a woman. When she's wanted. When she's loved.*

The Woman We Create

What is interesting is that cutting across all age groups men in general see a woman as womanly in terms of her involvement with a man—when she is loved by a man, when she is having sex with a man, when a man admires her, even when she is manipulating or dominating a man. To most men womanliness is not a quality in itself but a reflective attitude, a reaction to men. It follows then that a woman cannot be womanly when she is alone for there is nothing to reflect her womanliness.

Womanliness, to most men, does not exist as an innate quality of women, but is called forth by the men around them, a dormant quality awakened and brought to life by their presence. This reflects very accurately the way men have seen women through all of recorded history: women exist only in terms of men. They bear men's children, keep men's homes, service men's sexual desires and, from time to time, act as idols for men to worship, or scapegoats to blame for whatever goes wrong.

Even the women saw themselves in these roles, as functions of men. *I am womanly when I am needed by a man. When a man loves me. To be admired by a man.*

It seems strange, perhaps a betrayal of their own sex, for women to think this way, and yet they play a game in which men have set the rules. They live in a land where men have written the laws. It would be unnatural for them to believe that perhaps they themselves follow the attitudes that men have imposed on them.

The fact that some few women have seen through the attitudes of the society is the truly surprising thing. It is only a few who have, though a growing few. Women's Liberation represents only a very small fraction of all women, and women themselves are among the most vigorous enemies of Women's Lib.

It is an innate part of man's adjustment to his society that he see women as alive, human and reactive only in terms of his own needs. Our entire culture is predicated on this fact. In answering our questionnaire a typical man of the pre-World War II years states that he feels manly when he accomplishes a difficult task, that a man's chief characteristic is "doing his own thing without fear of any kind." But the same man sees woman's chief characteristic as dependence and the quality that makes her womanly as softness. He might well be talking about two different species of creature, not two sexes of the same creature.

But what he says and believes reflects the state of the world he lives in. His role is to accomplish a difficult task, to go out to a job each day, to work either with his body or with his brain at a job that by definition of the economic system must exploit him. And then he must struggle home by way of some inadequate transportation system to his wife and children.

He lives with the constant threat of the loss of his job in the economically shifty shadow of a chaotic system, sees the money he makes become less and less able to support his family and faces, at home, children who have only contempt for the world he fights in.

This is the typical man of today, and when he comes home from the outside world, a world that does not appreciate him, that grinds him down with gleeful certainty, he faces the bleak prospect of his own family.

What he would like, above all, is a wife unaffected by the society, unspoiled, unchanged, a wife who is all the domestic images presented by Hollywood in the forties and fifties, Doris Day, Debbie Reynolds and June Allyson, beautifully dressed and soft and clean and womanly and welcoming and understanding and sympathetic and calculated to rub off all the prickly burrs of an empty, hostile day.

This was the wife who had the dinner waiting, the children under control, the house immaculate and the hearth fire burning even when there was no hearth. This is what he wants and needs, for hasn't he been told in stories and movies that this is what marriage is all about? Hasn't he been led to expect it with every commercial on television, every *Reader's Digest* anecdote, every little stone that has helped build our culture?

Sure he expects it, he wants it and in his heart he knows that this is the role women should play. This is what he was promised since he first learned to focus his eyes.

And the odd thing, the fantastic thing, is that be believes this promise in spite of the fact that he has been brought up with the direct opposite of the promise. He has seen his own parents live out lives that give the lie to the Great American Dream that has nourished him. He knows that bitterness, hatred and resentment are all normal within a family, and yet he is still stupid enough, blind enough, or perhaps human enough to accept and expect the promise: women exist only in terms of himself. She is called into being at his wish, his will, his command. She is eternally the sleeping beauty waiting to be awakened by his kiss. The deep symbolism of the fairy tale has never left him.

And he comes home each night of his life—whether he is a middle-class executive, a salesman, storekeeper, adman, businessman or worker on an assembly line, a cop or construction worker or a ditch digger—with some variation of the American Dream. He climbs the stairs to his cramped apartment or walks the driveway to his smart suburban home with that same expectation. "She will be waiting to comfort me and assuage me. She will come to life when I smile at her and she will be a woman in terms of my need, my desire."

Woman in the Movies

Is this extreme? Are we men really this naive? Don't we understand women at all?

It isn't, we are and we don't. Look at our movies, for example. The only recent one I can recall that makes some attempt to see women as human is the film of D. H. Lawrence's *Women in Love*. At the end of the film Gudrun rejects her lover Gerald to find herself as a woman, as pointed a statement on woman's humanity as our screen has shown in a long time.

And yet, four out of five people, men and women, queried about the movie told me, "What a bitch, what an emasculating bitch Gudrun was." There is nothing surprising in this reaction. The woman who refuses to subdue herself, to debase herself, is less than woman. She has no right to exist in terms of her own wants, her own desires. Her role is to exist in terms of her man.

In *Women in Love* when Gerald cannot bend Gudrun to his will, cannot force her to exist in terms of himself, he attempts first to subdue her sexually in a scene that is terrifying in its brutal treatment of the sex act. He throws himself into her violently with all the weight of his body and without feeling as she screams with pain. But even this does not subdue her and in the end Gerald commits suicide rather than face his failure as a man.

An earlier scene in the film, a nude wrestling scene between the two men, Gerald and Rupert, plays with a latent homosexual relationship, not so much a physical homosexuality—though the wrestling scene is extremely physical —but a homosexuality of the mind, a common enough fantasy among men in this culture. Like Al, the construction worker who finds companionship only from other men, the fantasy goes, "I can be better friends with men than with women. Truer friends, closer friends, deeper friends."

In the very discerning and very sad movie, *Husbands*, one of the characters put it very plainly. "Except for sex, and my wife's very good at sex, I like you guys better."

"You guys" are two other husbands. The three men, Harry, Gus and Archie, have come from the funeral of a fourth friend. Suddenly faced with mortality, they can't bear to return to their wives. Instead, searching for the reassurance of sex and physical intimacy, the three set out together on a mammoth binge that takes them from a bar in Manhattan across the ocean to Europe. The love and intimacy they need, the warmth of another body to ward off the inevitable and now inimical cold of the grave, is something they don't even consider finding with their wives.

They huddle together at first and then turn to strangers at a bar and brief pick-ups in England—anything to avoid the deadly trap of their suburban lives, their wives and children. Back there lie only sterility, loneliness and, as we see in one brief scene, absolute alienation. Harry's wife tells him, "I'm just not comfortable with you, Harry." A bitter hateful cry wrung out of her very soul.

Even the women the men pick up are wrong. The only right relationships, the only relationships that will work— if it weren't for that damnable sex thing, for these men are not homosexual—is the company of the three of them.

The Company of Men

We are more comfortable together than we are with our wives. We are happiest together, more satisfied, and yet we belong to our wives, not to each other. This is the basic theme of *Husbands*. Nor is this an isolated theme. It occurs in Lawrence at the turn of the century and in Cassavetes in 1970. Tennessee Williams toyed with it in *Cat on a Hot Tin Roof.*

Brick, talking about his wife Maggie, tells Big Daddy, "Y'know, I think that Maggie had always felt sort of left out because she and me never got any closer together than two people just get in bed, which is not much closer than two cats on a—fence humping . . ." Skipper, his fellow football player, was the one Brick was really close to, and again it was the company of men that mattered most.

Hemingway, too, sings the company of men and again and again it appears in meaningful fiction, in fiction written by men. Men are companionship for intellectual satisfaction, for all the ennobling virtues. And women?

In *My Fair Lady*, Henry Higgins sums it up, "Why can't a woman be more like a man?"

What is it that draws men together? Why, in our society, do men find more pleasure in each other's company than in the company of women? Why do so many American husbands hunger for a night out with the boys? Why are there men's clubs whose halls are so restricted that women must use separate lobbies, as they do in New York City's Yale Club? Why are hunting parties so exclusively male? Why are there bars that are for men only? Why do even children form clubs for boys only, "Girl Haters" societies? What is this strange phenomenon among men, this need to cluster in groups and exclude women? Is it, as Williams writes in his play, ". . . because we had a finer thing between us?" Is the company of men finer, purer?

Coming from the uncertain masculinity of Williams we are not sure, but when someone with the aggressive masculinity of Norman Mailer says, during a television interview with Orson Welles, "that women should be kept in cages," we begin to wonder about even a "real" man's view of women. Mailer explained, "We respect the lions in the zoo, but we want them kept in cages, don't we?" But this explanation hardly takes the edge off the statement. Women are dangerous. Women are a race apart. Treat them with respect and, if you can, screw them, but be sure you can always return to the company of men—a finer, more decent company.

Why?

Lionel Tiger, in his book *Men in Groups,* bases his explanation on evolutionary roots. "Why do human males form all male groups?" Tiger asks, and then hypothesizes that "the behavior of men in groups in part reflects an underlying biologically transmitted propensity with roots in human evolutionary history."

In other words, men form groups, clubs, teams, all-male gatherings of one sort or another because it is part of their heredity to do so. As proof of this he attempts to show, with animal groups, that male bonding, as he calls the tendency to form male groups, existed before man. He describes bonding in baboons where three males will often band together against other males in the group to strengthen their own status. Unfortunately for his thesis, he doesn't find male bonding in many other animal species, or in many primate species.

In primitive humans, Tiger emphasizes the importance of hunting as a way of life and the need to rely on other men while hunting. Because of woman's concern with children and her weaker physical state, hunting became a man's province. "My proposition," Tiger says, "is that specialization for hunting widened the gap between the behavior of males and females. It favored those 'genetic packages' which arranged matters so that males hunted cooperatively in groups while females engaged in maternal and some gathering activities."

He suggests that this male-to-male link for hunting purposes became programmed into man's life cycle. Those men who tended to hunt in groups had a better chance of succeeding at the hunt and therefore a better chance of surviving. This tendency toward forming male groups or bonds therefore gave the men who had it to the greatest degree an edge over their brothers in the genetic race. It seems logical that natural selection would eventually seize on this bonding pattern and weave it into the chromosomes of men. When hunting was no longer necessary for survival, the bonding pattern would still persist.

Tiger goes on from this premise to some fascinating if questionable conclusions. He sees male bonding as a very strong force in modern politics and law, which, he says, "represents the cumulative decision-making and tradition of the dominant males." He also notes how few women are involved in politics and sees this lack of involvement as a function of womanliness, while man's involvement is a function of manliness. He points out that "those parties most concerned with female issues and rights perversely receive the lesser share of the female vote."

He also cites the grouping together of men in business as a hangover of this built-in or programmed bonding instinct. And of course there is war, which he notes is almost universally an all-male enterprise.

Initiations and secret societies, men's exclusive clubs and the "finer relationship between men," Tiger's work would indicate, all stem from this basic bonding situation. If this is so, then the way in which men see women, their estimate of womanliness, must be carefully reexamined in the light of male bonding.

How Do Men See Women?

Purpose: To force the man to confront his deepest prejudices about the opposite sex.

Round one: While the man watches, the woman takes two male dolls and puts them together. She pretends they are in a bar or on a park bench or in a fishing boat a mile off shore. Speaking for both of them she has them describe her female friends.

Round two: While the woman watches, the man takes the two male dolls and plays the same game, again describing how he and his male friends really see the female friends of the woman.

3

The Bad Woman

Return to the Womb

If we are to consider what men believe are womanly traits and, in a broader sense, how men see women, we should logically start with the way men see their mothers, for our mother is the first woman we know. This is fertile ground, so fertile that it reminds me of the story of the farmer who was being sold some new acreage. "Is it fertile?" the seller asked. "Why, drop in the seed and jump back or you'll be hit by the growing plant."

Freud becomes the logical whipping boy when there is any discussion of motherhood or, for that matter, of women. What many people find hard to accept is the fact that Freud laid the groundwork for most modern psychiatric male chauvinism. It isn't so much that he found women different from men that troubles us; rather it is the quality of the difference.

"To be loved is a stronger need for them (women) than to love," he stated in a lecture delivered late in his career, in 1932. He questioned women's ability to respond sexually, noting that while the sexual frigidity of women is sometimes psychogenic and in that case can be influenced or changed, "[i]n other cases it suggests the hypothesis of its being constitutionally determined and even of there being a contributory anatomical factor." In other words, they're just not made the way we are, they don't feel what we feel. Shades of Nietzsche, who before the turn of the century emphasized that a man must always think of women as Orientals do: "He must conceive of women as a possession, a property that can be locked, as something predestined for service and achieving her perfection in that."

To give credit where it's due, Freud made us all aware that women are different, mysterious and strange. But he never forgot that she was also hostile. It is the hostility of women that concerned Freud to an obsessive degree, and of course his concern was an early recognition of the basic incompatibility of the sexes.

But he wasn't completely against women, as so many of his critics maintain. In speaking of women's genitals, he declared, "this uncanny place is nothing but the entrance to the old home of mankind, to that abode where every one of us was once and first at home." Freud goes on to see a woman's vagina, therefore, as somehow strange, frightening and threatening.

I cannot read his description without thinking of Barney, an old drinking friend of mine in my premarital days. Barney, a truck driver, was unmarried too and had very few hang-ups about his role in relation to women. "What I like is pussy," Barney explained to me once. "It's warm and comfortable and a place where I belong. Maybe I'm sorry I crawled out to begin with, but God damn it, I'm going to spend the rest of my life trying to crawl back in!"

Barney's credo can be easily related to some current analytic theory—Ferenczi, as quoted by Karen Horney in *The Flight from Womanhood,* comes up with what she labeled "an extremely brilliant genital theory." He concluded that the "real incitement to coitus, its true ultimate meaning for both sexes, is to be sought in the desire to return to the mother's womb."

Freud, exploring the mother-child relationship, decided that boy-children fear being killed by their mothers and respond with what he characterizes as "aggressive oral and sadistic wishes." Many psychiatrists can't buy this type of thinking. Neither can I. Is this really how men see women? I think it becomes a matter of interpretation.

Barney's desire to "get into" women was based on his sensual enjoyment of the act of "screwing." So it is with all men. If there were no stimulation of the nerve endings in the tips of our penises, no culmination of that stimulation in the ecstasy of orgasm, we would probably not bother to have sex at all except for procreation. Then what would happen to all those subtle desires to punish our mother, to return to the womb? Would we still have all the elements present in today's man-woman situation? Would we still have this eternal conflict? If we did, I would take any odds that we would not resolve it or attempt to resolve it through sexual intercourse.

And yet this basic fact seems neglected by psychiatrist after psychiatrist. Following Freud, they still spell out relationships between mother and son and interpret sexual interaction in terms of those relationships.

| 43

Beware the Vagina Dentata

Karen Horney, who is generally considered more progressive than Freud, took a swipe at mothers in what seems to me a far-out concept, that little boys are threatened because their penises are so small and their mothers' vaginas are so big. In *The Dread of Women* she wrote that this aroused a fear of ridicule which she found occurring in the man. Of course, even if it is far-out, I suppose it isn't much different than Freud's penis envy, to which, in a way, it's a female psychiatrist's reply. As Norman Mailer put it, it is "pussy envy."

Between Horney's time and now the attack on mothers has gone on. In the 1950s Suzanne Reichard and Carl Tillman, in the *Journal of Psychiatry*, came up with the term "schizophrenogenic mother," the mother who at once rejects and seduces her child.

In that same decade, a fertile time for anti-momism, René Spitz also found the mother at fault. On the one hand, according to Spitz, she held back and didn't give her child the proper experiences and on the other hand she poisoned what experiences she gave him. The roster of psychiatric researchers who fell into line to put Mom down is a long one, including women as well as men—Margaret Gerard and Margaret Mehler and Louise Despert and Melitta Sperling and Adelaide Johnson, and on and on. The mother, as she was seen by all of these writers, men and women, was the villain in the picture.

But mom as the villain was in no way pecuilar to the

fifties. Historically, and prehistorically in mankind's oldest myths, mothers and all women were seen by men as dangerous, debilitating and deadly. It is not chance that an Orthodox Jewish daily prayer goes: "I thank thee Oh Lord that you have not created me a woman." Women were less than a second sex to Orthodox Jews in the old days. The girl-child was a downright misfortune.

And lest we indict the Jews alone, consider a few proverbs from other people. The Portuguese: Do not trust a good woman and keep away from the bad ones. How like the schizophrenogenic mother who can't win either way. The Germans: Whenever a woman dies there is one less quarrel on earth. Or the Greeks: The slave is entirely without the faculty of deliberation; the female possesses it but in a form which remains inconclusive. Or to touch religion. Job, in the Old Testament, asks, "How can he be clean that is born of a woman?" And St. Paul, in the New Testament, says, "Let the woman learn in silence with all subjection."

Things never looked too good for women—as men saw them. And even that part of women that all men were willing to take a chance with didn't appear too healthy a spot.

In the early forties, writing in the *British Journal of Medical Psychiatry*, Verrier Elwin discussed the *vagina dentata legend*, a legend that seems almost universal and reflects one male view of women as castration threats in general. According to the legend there may be hidden teeth in a woman's vagina, and the unwary man who ventures in runs the risk of bad toothmarks and a chewed-up penis at best and of losing his manhood at the worst. Elwin cites East Indian legends of unwary men who take their chances with toothed vaginas and lose their best parts. There are also heroes who extract the teeth or break them off.

The legend appears in other countries besides India and reflects man's often expressed view that woman is a threat and a danger, not just in a psychological way but in a very real physical way. Or are the legends simply reflections of that part of men that dislikes women and sees womanliness as something distasteful and abhorrent, then justifies his dislike with legend?

But the legends are so universal. Consider Samson being done in by Delilah, being shorn of his strength with his hair. Woman is the beloved and yet the betrayer. She cannot love without betrayal. Salome, being rejected by John the Baptist, demands his head, "If I cannot have you living, I will take you dead." The Medusa who turns men to stone, the Circe who turns them into beasts, the Sphinx who killed them when they couldn't guess her riddles, the harpies and the furies of Ancient Greece—there is no end in legend to the terrible woman, the vengeful woman, the threatening woman, the frightening, and emasculating woman, and the legends even appear in primitive cultures untouched by ours.

Emasculation: Learning a Defense

Purpose: To help the man confront his own fears of being emasculated by a woman, while at the same time helping the woman to understand why so many men have these fears.

The man takes the female doll and calls it BALLBREAKER. The woman takes the male doll and calls it MAN. The man, impersonating BALLBREAKER plays the lead role.

The situation: BALLBREAKER is a woman out to destroy MAN. She can be any woman, out of the man's past or someone he now knows. They invent

their own situation and dialogue but the nub of the situation must be BALL-BREAKER attempting to destroy MAN. MAN (played by the woman) defends himself.

In round two the roles are reversed and, based on what he has learned as BALLBREAKER, the man takes the lead as MAN.

Is Woman All This Bad?

Bronislaw Malinowski in *The Sexual Life of Savages* tells of a native South Sea Island legend of an island full of sexually insatiable women so rabid in their desire for intercourse that they sexually misused any unlucky man cast on their shores and even misused their own children, if boys, to the point of death.

The frightening part of this story is the attitude it reflects of man's fear of women. Is woman all this bad? Do we men really see her like this? And do we see ourselves as August Strindberg, the playwright, saw men? According to him the man she opposes is ". . . the true Lord of the world who created civilization, spread the blessings of culture, who fathered all the great thoughts, the arts, the professions, all that is great and beautiful in the world. . . ."

I suppose it's no wonder that we men are so indignant that we see women as such a threat and fury when they oppose all these wonderful things.

But is this truly how men have always seen women? Are

hurricanes even today named after women for just these attributes? Is womanliness, then, as it is reflected from the mirror of men, frightening, threatful, emasculating, ready to attack and kill us if we step out of line, if we give the wrong answer, if we even gaze at her openly?

It would be a promising situation if we could say no, if we could put the toothed vagina, the destroying woman, the earth mother, in the distant past and say, "We've come a long way, baby. We don't see women as a threat any more. Today's women are simply another side of the coin called humanity. A man is as incomplete without a woman as a woman is without a man. As for a threat, does the head of a coin see the tail as a threat?"

And yet it was only thirty years ago that Philip Wylie in his *Generation of Vipers* put mothers down completely and devastatingly. The quality of womanliness as he saw it was voracious and destructive: "Disguised as good old mom, dear old mom, sweet old mom, your loving mom, and so on, she is the bride at every funeral and the corpse at every wedding."

As Wylie looked at mom then, so do a score of modern novelists look at her now. Philip Roth does her in in *Portnoy's Complaint* and so does Bruce Jay Friedman in *A Mother's Kisses*. And in case we think it's only a function of Jewish culture, there's Tom McHale, who in *Farragan's Retreat* totally destroyed the dear old Irish mother, and, of course, Eugene O'Neill a while back in *Long Day's Journey into Night* gave her another working over. In fact she's fair game for just about every male author in and out of fiction. Wolfgang Lederer in *The Fear of Women* talks of her voice, calling it rasping, brassy and unctuous all at the same time: "It drowns out all other conversation and rises triumphantly and unmistakably over the murmur of restaurants and the roar of airports all over the globe."

Of course mom was the first woman in a man's life. Whatever she arouses in him of love or hate, envy or bitterness, admiration or anger, will almost inevitably be directed toward other women, toward those women he becomes involved with sexually and in other ways, and eventually toward the one woman he marries. Or as it often happens to upper-middle-class men, toward all those women he marries.

Above All We Use Her

Ortega y Gasset, the Spanish philosopher, writing of women said, "The core of the feminine mind, no matter how intelligent the woman may be, is occupied by an irrational power."

Irrational power becomes another term for the inner mystery. There is something in a woman men just do not know and cannot know and perhaps can never know. There are vast depths to women, tranquil and dark, and there are also deadly, dangerous places, tooth-filled vaginas. She is the everlasting filler of our needs, an object to be cherished and at the same time used. We have, since the dawn of history, enslaved her and dominated her, used her and yet feared her. We see her in all these ways. We love her and we hate her and, oh Lord, how we fear her! And *above all we use her*. For so many of us men this is womanliness, the use of a woman to satisfy a need.

Every man fantasizes situations in which he has complete power over a woman, but can we all handle this fantasy of power? If we had it, how would we handle it?

The Ultimate Power

Purpose: To give the man a chance to act out one of the most common male fantasies, and discover how he feels about it.

The man takes the male doll and calls him MAN. The woman takes the female doll and names it WOMAN. In this game MAN has complete and absolute power over WOMAN. She can do nothing to oppose him, in fact, she doesn't want to oppose him. She is his adoring slave.

The scene is a dimly lighted, over-decorated bedroom. The scenario is left up to MAN. Anything goes.

What to watch for in this scene: Given his own way, is MAN tenderly concerned about her responses or rapacious? A joyous libertine or a hung-up sadist? Or does he cop out, overwhelmed by the realization of so strong a sexual fantasy?

Sexual Sharing

In terms of using women I am reminded of a recent radio program I heard, a group discussion about new forms of marriage, with representatives of two generations, the over-forties and the under-thirties. At one point in the discussion one of the men was asked how he would feel if his twenty-one-year-old daughter moved into a communal marriage situation.

"Suppose," the moderator said, "she came to you and said, 'Dad, I want to go and live in this apartment. There are three men and two other girls and we don't want to get married. We just want to live together and share.'"

"Share sexually?" the father asked.

"That's right. A new kind of arrangement: sexual sharing. What would your reaction be to your daughter if she said this? Now honestly, how would you react?" the moderator asked.

"My immediate reaction? I'd faint! Then I'd start yelling!"

Now this man had shown by his earlier remarks that he was not only honest but liberal. Still it was asking a great deal of him to take this. The moderator then asked, "Would you be afraid of her getting pregnant?"

"Well, no. Not with the pill. She's on it anyway."

"Is it the relationship of your daughter to just any of the men? Is this what bugs you? The incestuous aspect? The moral aspect?"

"Moral? No." He hesitated, then he said, "I think it's the feeling that she'd be used in that kind of a situation. The three men would just be using her, and that would hurt me more than anything else."

The moderator said, "I can see that, but let me ask you another question. I'd like you to answer in all honesty. Tell me, how would you feel if your teen-age son—what is he, nineteen—were involved in the same situation? If he came to you and said, 'Hey, Dad, me and two other guys, we're sharing this apartment with three girls.'"

The father laughed and said, "In all honesty I'd have only one reaction, Wow! What a great situation for the kid!"

I never heard a clearer explanation of the double standard. A woman, no matter what the sexual situation, is something to be used. We object to an obvious use by someone else if the woman belongs to us. Otherwise we chuckle at the use, thinking, "Lucky man." We wish we were in his shoes.

Triple Play: Miller to Mailer to Millett

As men, this same envious wish fills us when we read some of Henry Miller's work. In his perceptive essay, "Promiscuity and the Casanova Impulse," Colin Wilson calls Miller a scrounger whose chief motivation seems to be the desire for a quick undignified poke. "His talent," Wilson says, "exceeds his self-belief and therefore his seriousness as an artist. This lack of self-confidence is almost synonymous with mendacity."

But there is, curiously or perhaps naturally enough, an excess of self-confidence in Miller's descriptions of sex. Self-confidence in his case leads to contempt for the woman he uses, and use her he does. In *The Tropic of Capricorn* he describes an experience with an amnesic deaf-mute girl, obviously the best kind of woman to use for she can't remember anything better than the present sexual incident. Nor can she spoil it all by talking at the wrong time. Miller described his encounter with the girl as if the two of them were just a couple of quiet maniacs working away in the dark like gravediggers. "It was a fucking Paradise and I knew it, and I was ready to fuck my brains away if necessary. She was probably the best fuck I ever had. She never once opened her trap—not that night nor the next nor any night."

Miller has found his ultimate heaven. Not only the woman who can be used easily—she comes to him in the dark as soon as she smells his odor—but also the woman who never opens her trap. She is a deaf-mute so there is no possibility that she will tell him he was right or wrong. There's no chance of her criticizing him. He doesn't need criticism for that matter, for he is only using her. What is right or wrong to the object we use.

Let's ignore the morality of the encounter. What is so revealing in this episode is Miller's view of womanliness. Even if it is only one aspect of womanliness, it is still a desirable aspect, the best aspect of all. "One out of a million," as he says. His dream of women is use. Miller, in spite of all his brave profanity and bold sexual showmanship, has never really grown up in the sense that he has never given up the idea that all women are a reflection of his own mother, the one who nurtured and protected him and satisfied all his needs. He has never discarded the idea that women are only to satisfy his needs.

Kate Millett, whetting her own axe in her book *Sexual Politics,* sees the sadistic implication in Miller's writing as uppermost, along with his need to degrade women and uplift men. In discussing Miller's treatment of Ida Verlaine in *Sexus,* she says, "His penis is now an instrument of chastisement, whereas Ida's genitalia are but the means of her humiliation." She goes on to note that "each moment absorbs him further and degrades her lower."

But Millett cites Miller's fantasy of sexual dominance as part of all men's need to dominate women. It is her thesis that sex is deep at the heart of our trouble. "Unless we eliminate the most pernicious of our systems of oppression, unless we go to the very center of the sexual politic and its sick delirium of power and violence, all our efforts at liberation will but land us again in the primordial stews," Millett says.

But what is the center of the sexual politic? Millett looks at the symptoms and sees them as the cause. The effort of man to dominate woman is not the cause of the struggle between the sexes, it is not the cause of the basic incompatibility of men and women. Rather it is the result of that incompatibility.

In *The Prisoner of Sex,* Norman Mailer, in a spate of verbal diarrhea, hacked Kate Millett to shreds for her attack on Henry Miller and used her misquotation of Miller as fuel to his indignant mayhem. But Millett didn't do a great deal of misquoting or misinterpreting. For example, in one section she quoted Miller describing sex: ". . . he pulled out for a second, as though to cool his cock off: . . . and shoved a big long carrot up her twat." In taking a swipe at Millett, Mailer gives the proper quote and fills in those three dots: ". . . he pulled out for a second, as though to cool his cock off and then very slowly and gently he shoved a big carrot up her twat." The exclusion of slowly and gently, Mailer says indignantly, is because "Millett didn't want to weaken her indictment by qualifying the force of the shove."

I hold that a carrot is a carrot and the humility of having it shoved into a woman's vagina is hardly lessened by the gentleness of the shove.

What Mailer is really torn off about is Millett's criticism of his own *American Dream,* a novel in which at the climax the hero murders his wife and "buggers" her maid. Mailer disposes of Millett's criticism of his book in a few brief paragraphs and then takes after her for her criticism of Miller. But Mailer's view of women is so strikingly like Miller's that we inevitably begin to wonder about *An American Dream* and why he doesn't really answer Millett's arguments except to claim that she has misinterpreted analingus for sodomy.

These fine sexual distinctions take nothing away from Millett's contention that Mailer holds woman in contempt and feels that man must dominate her. I wish Mailer had stuck to the point, admitted what he feels about women and then proceeded to explain it instead of muddying up the water with his defense of Miller.

What emerges from the Mailer-Miller-Millett debacle is a growing conviction that men do indeed regard women as created to be dominated or used. They see the quality of womanliness as an ability to be used by men and, what is more, they believe that women take joy in that use.

It may well be that some women do enjoy it. In any event there is truth in what George Bernard Shaw wrote in his preface to *Getting Married:* "Women are called womanly only when they regard themselves as existing solely for the use of men." Called womanly by men, that is.

What did the men who answered our questions say about womanliness? *A woman is womanly when she has a man. When she is wanted. Sex fulfills her. Being made love to by a man.* It's basically true. She is considered a woman only when she services men.

4

The Mirror of Venus:
Women Look at Women

What Does a Woman Want?

Sally lives alone in a small studio apartment in Chicago. Single, attractive and still in her thirties, Sally has a good job in the offices of a local real estate company, and she has a very active social life.

"Actually I go out with three different men," Sally laughs. "But each gives me something different. With Jim it's intellectual, we can talk forever, and with Dan it's all action, skiing in the winter, water sports in the summer—he has a boat on the lake—horseback riding. Dan is great fun, and with George, well with George it's very physical. Dancing, dinner and sex. I enjoy sex with George. Womanly? I guess it does make me feel womanly, except—well, when I think about it I don't know how I really feel. I have an uncomfortable idea that George is using me, really using me, and that bothers me.

"No, if I told the truth I wouldn't say George makes me feel womanly. He makes me feel cheapened somehow, used. Oh, I know I'm using him too, but that makes it even worse. I don't want to marry George, or Dan or Jim because why would marriage change things? I'd still feel used, still feel a little less than a whole person."

Sex, although Sally enjoys it, does not make her feel like a woman. In fact, Sally is hard-pressed to put her finger on just what does make her feel like a woman. "Perhaps," she says thoughtfully, "I never have been sure of my own womanhood."

Celia, like Sally, is uncertain of just what makes her a woman. Married and with two small children, running to fat at thirty, Celia considers herself a poor housekeeper and perhaps not much of a wife. "Everything overwhelms me, the house, the meals, the babies—when Hal comes home at night my work is never finished. Supper is never ready, I'm always at my wit's end, and invariably we end up quarreling. Half the time Hal takes over and gets supper on the table. I just can't cope with things, and then I feel worse, guilty because he's worked all day and now he does my job.

"Womanly? Hell, I don't even feel human. I'm not even sure I love Hal and the kids. I suppose if I had to describe what makes me womanly I'd say, let me get through one day with everything going right and I'd be a woman that day, and a human being too, if there's any difference."

Like Celia and Sally, Dotty is also uncertain of her own womanhood. She and Peter live in the suburbs of a small Western city. Their three sons are just midway through their teens, and all aspects of Dotty's life seem to center around the man's world of Peter and the boys. Dotty, a tall, raw-boned woman of forty, has always considered herself awk-

ward and plain and never got over her surprise when Peter
asked her to marry him.

"Keeping our house feminine has been the hardest job
in my marriage," Dotty says. "Keeping myself feminine is
even harder."

What makes you feminine? What makes you womanly?

"Womanly?" Dotty spreads her hands, encompassing the
house. "That's easy. Being a mother. Knowing the boys de-
pend on me. Taking care of Peter, cooking, cleaning, sewing, being a balance for the family . . . oh yes, and making
Peter think he's really the balance."

There is a long pause, and then with considerable bitterness, "I don't know what makes me feel womanly in all
honesty. Most of the time I don't even think I feel like a
woman. I feel more like a drudge without a wage, and yet
I love my husband and the boys. I love my home too,
only . . ."

Only what?

"Only I wish I could throw it all over. I wish I weren't
convinced that the only way I can earn Peter's love is by
being a little Connie Casserole! I wish, just once, I could
do something that mattered, something important. I wish
I could amount to something, count for something, make
some kind of mark on this earth."

You're not doing that now?

"Oh, I don't know. Sometimes I feel I'm doing it by being
a mother and a housewife, and then, just as often—maybe
more often—I hate it all. What a waste! Now that I think of
it, you want to know what womanliness is to me? Womanliness is a waste, a big meaningless waste, for all the cooking, cleaning and sewing. Nobody wants it or needs it.
Peter and the boys would be just as happy without it all,

and they'd never notice if it were gone. No, it's all a waste, and that's being a woman."

That is being a woman for thousands of housewives like Dotty. On the surface they tell themselves that their life is meaningful and that the work they do has significance, that they are an integral and necessary part of society, and yet, deep down, they wonder. Sometimes the wonder is not so deep. Scratch the surface of the happy, suburban or the well-adjusted city housewife and you find a doubting or discontented woman.

Defining Her Needs

Purpose: To help both the man and the woman work out the answer to the question, "What does this woman want from me?"

For this game the woman selects a female doll and as many male dolls as she chooses to surround the female doll. The female doll is named ME. The male dolls are named HUSBAND, LOVER, FATHER, SON, TEACHER, BOSS or whatever, and are all played by the man.

Each male doll offers ME his idea of what he believes will make her happy. ME is then free to react in any way, from absolute fury to genuine pleasure.

Is the Mad Housewife Really Mad?

In her recent novel, *Diary of a Mad Housewife*, Sue Kaufman brings out this discontent beautifully. The motion picture based on the novel exaggerated the relationship of the husband and wife, emphasizing all the areas of disagreement and discontent, but in doing so it turned the husband into a caricature and allowed the men in the audience to laugh at him and say rather smugly, "We're not like that at all."

And yet the petulance of the husband, his arrogance and unreasonable demands, his constant shaming of his wife in front of their children, faded into insignificance in the face of the peculiar acceptance of all this by the wife.

Carrie Snodgress, playing the part of the wife in the movie version, was mad only in the sense that she moved through an insane world without adjustment, for madness in the final analysis is an inability to adjust to reality. Carrie moved through the film with a wounded look and seemed to live in a world of her own that only occasionally touched the real world.

But what caused the wound? Some vital part of herself was cut out. We are not at all sure if it was done by the constant attacks of her husband or if the attacks are due to the loss of some vital essence. Is the essence womanliness? Or is the essence independence? Is it the ability to react to life and does womanliness entail losing this essence?

What would make the housewife a real woman? What is missing, or if she is a real woman, what has she lost? She thinks it may be sex, that she may have lost her ability to function as a woman on a sexual level, and she drifts into an extramarital affair to find out.

The man she chooses wants sex only as a physical relief. He wants no involvement, and up to a point this satisfies the housewife. But there is a quality within her—womanliness?—which cannot settle for sex alone in a relationship.

Characteristically she achieves her freedom from the affair with the realization that her lover is not a complete man.

We have also been shown that her husband is not a complete man—whatever manliness may be. The housewife is left, in the end, with nothing. She cannot accept what being a woman means in our society, taking care of the house and children with absolute efficiency and dealing with a husband who has never reached emotional, sexual or functional maturity. At one point he loses their life savings in a wild and foolish investment.

Nor can she make any valid attachment outside of marriage. The other man is as immature in his way as her husband. It is just a matter of a deeper trap.

The Feminine Time Machine

There is no solution for the mad, middle-class housewife within the framework of our society. For her, womanliness boils down to one thing—complete subordination to a man. But what else is there to womanliness? What is a real woman if there is such a thing? What makes a woman feel womanly?

In the first chapter we took a look at "a typical American couple out of television prime time by way of *Reader's Digest.*" We looked at Joe and Ann and found that here there was no question of womanliness. Ann felt completely womanly and subjected herself to Joe, indeed getting most of the satisfaction necessary to make her a woman who can fulfill the classic role of housewife.

But the Mad Housewife couldn't subject herself and still

feel like a woman, or for that matter even like a human being. In the last scene of the movie we see her in a group therapy session trying to deal with her madness, and one of the male group members explodes with fury at her even trying to seek help. "Here's this dame who's got everything, a fancy apartment, a husband with a good job, kids, nothing to do with herself—and she cheats behind her husband's back and complains!" In essence, this man is expressing society's viewpoint.

Is she a rare exception? Take our other two housewives, Celia and Dotty. Celia had a husband who helped her, and yet she felt less a woman because of it. And Dotty equated womanliness with waste. Are Celia and Dotty rare exceptions?

Question a thousand Celias and Dottys and see what comes up. Do any of them feel womanly because they have taken on the role of housewife? Is this what is wrong with unmarried Sally? What does make a woman feel like a woman? What comes across, as you ask more and more women this question, is that this womanly feeling is very much a matter of generation. Femininity rides a strange time machine. Most American women seem to divide naturally into four groups, the young ones under thirty, the group that ranges from thirty to forty-five, those between forty-five and sixty, and the oldest bunch, the women over sixty.

The edges of these groups are not hard, and there is considerable overlapping. *What seems to determine a group is not so much the age of the women in it as the periods during which these women reached maturity, and the periods during which they were children.* Humans tend to become frozen into tight patterns of thinking and behavior during their early childhood years. Once in such a pattern or mold it takes the heat generated by a cataclysm to un-mold and remold them. It can happen, but it doesn't happen often.

The young group, those under thirty, are all post-World War II women, born in the final years of the war or after it. As Margaret Mead said, they are the only natives in this world: "All of us who grew up before World War II are pioneers, immigrants in time who have left behind our familiar worlds to live in a new age . . ." She is right. We who came of age in those pre-war years matured in another era, in another time with different folkways and mores, different values, goals and ambitions, a different set of rights and wrongs.

We like to think that we were as alienated from our parents as this generation is from its parents, but the jump is much greater. With all the generations before the war there was a quantitative difference between parent and child. We were all a bit freer than our parents, and they were a bit freer than their parents. With the post-war generation, the difference became qualitative. The people under thirty, those who lived their childhood in the 1950s and matured in the 1960s, particularly the late 1950s, are a different breed, almost a different species of man and woman—particularly woman.

The old dos and don'ts no longer apply, and there is an entirely different set of values and ideals. "We are the only generation," an eighteen-year-old girl told me recently, "who have grown up under the shadow of annihilation. We've always lived with the bomb and the knowledge of its power to destroy, and now that we've finally come to accept the knowledge of that destruction and live with its possibility, we face the ecological death of our planet, the ultimate pollution which only allows us some thirty-five more years. Is it any wonder we think differently?"

Whatever the reason, they do think differently, and perhaps with more freedom and honesty. The great majority of women under thirty, when asked what made them feel womanly, said acting as a woman in a biological sense. *Having a man's arms around me. A man's reaction to my body. Sexual intercourse. Knowing that I can arouse a man sexually.*

Sex: With or Without Love

The same thing may also evoke womanliness in some older women. A few of them said, *I feel like a woman when a man loves me* or *the love of a man turns me into a woman,* but there was less of a sense of sexuality the older the woman was. Over thirty, womanliness began to be equated with motherhood. *I feel like a woman in terms of my child. Motherhood makes me feel womanly. Taking care of my children.*

The acceptance of motherhood as a function of womanliness is logical, but the shift from sexuality to love is, I believe, less a function of age and fading libido than a reflection of the world of their youth and maturity. In the late 1930s and early 1940s women were taught that sexual love was carnal love. The girl who had sexual intercourse without being in love with the man was in some way cheapened, less of a woman and used by the man—the way Sally felt about sex with George. To have sex legitimatized, you had to tack it on to love. The really "decent" women not only tacked on love, but saw the entire process as love. The physical part of the act was rarely talked about. The spiritual part, the "love," became most important.

Today's young woman, like those in my sampling under thirty, can often accept sex alone as a worthwhile relationship. They can understand their own physical need for it and admit and satisfy that need. This isn't true of all of today's young women, of course. There are still hangovers from the beginning of the century. There are still girls who are so heavily influenced by their parent's thinking and values that they must equate love and sex, and there are still boys who feel only contempt for a girl they have had sex with. But these young people are few and growing fewer. The trend is toward the philosophy of those young people who accept sex as a valid act in itself.

Equal Time

Purpose: To help put the woman in touch with her sexual needs.

In many relationships, despite the new freedom, women cannot express their sexual needs to a man. They may be too inhibited or they may not even know what their own needs are.

The woman takes a female doll and calls it WOMAN. She then takes a male doll and calls it LOVER. She plays both roles while the man watches. She is in control of an ideal situation in which she will express to the man her own version of perfect love-making.

The scenario is left to the woman.

> **What to watch for: Given her own way, is WOMAN tenderly concerned about LOVER's responses, or is she selfish? Is she hostile, aggressive or submissive?**
>
> **It is important to play this scene spontaneously and not according to socially acceptable or idealized roles.**

But for the women in my sampling between thirty and forty-five, the sex act must be accompanied by love, and the love must come first. They can then feel womanly when they are loved, and indeed many can feel womanly without sex as long as they still have love.

In the next group, those women from forty-five to sixty, the "being loved" motif still remains, but more and more often the woman feels womanly if she loves someone, if she can do things for someone, take care of someone. *Keeping house for my husband makes me feel womanly. Caring for my children. Being looked to for help by those weaker than I* or even the Dear Abby syndrome, *Helping people solve their problems.*

For a number of women in this age group it's *Cooking, Cleaning, Making a home, Scrubbing the kitchen floor*— the house, the home, has become an end in itself. This may be an acceptance of a life style that allows no other acceptable outlet for a woman with a family, or it may be part of a built-in biological urge to be a homemaker. Whatever the cause, the vast majority of women in this age group have turned from physical love as an expression of womanliness to service. They are most womanly, they feel, when they are taking care of those they love.

Beyond sixty, in the last decades of life, the sense of

service spreads out beyond the family. *The love of my grandchildren. Caring for my friends. Being cared for. Being pampered by friends and family. Baking and cooking for the family and friends. Charity work. Being taken care of.* Womanliness becomes less and less a matter of relating to an individual male, and more and more a matter of relating to other people.

Love and the Senior Citizen

An interesting thread running through these older women's concepts of womanliness is the business of being pampered. Many of them, the older ones particularly, see being made a fuss over as truly feminine. This may well be a reflection of the time when they were young, when women, at the turn of the century, were considered womanly when they were treated like a pet or a precious toy. It may also, in part, be a return of their childish feelings, a foretaste of senility. There is for many women in these later years a sense of futility, of uselessness. *I feel neither womanly nor human for that matter. I think perhaps I've outlived my usefulness* is a common complaint in this age group.

Again, an answer to this attitude of uselessness may lie in the fact that these women date back to the turn of the century. Life in those days was a different matter. An older woman stayed at home, and most families had three or more generations living under one roof. The older women had their place. They were in contact with youth as well as middle age, and they knew that they were important, that their role in the family allowed more freedom to the younger people. There was never a problem of sitters with these built-in helpers, never a problem of too much work for the younger or middle generation. All work was spread out over the generations, and there were always secret recipes, secret cures, secret arts that the older women treasured and that increased her value to the family.

Today the situation is quite different, except in a few rural communities. In the vast majority of families the older folk live by themselves. The women over sixty are often widows who have outlived their husbands, often rattling around in large, empty houses or living lonely lives in city apartments. There is no question of their use. They know quite well that they are useless, but their formative years took place when women over sixty were useful. Why, they inevitably ask, are they different? And without any answer this question seems to exaggerate their loneliness.

The Feminine "Illusion"

A slightly different view of womanliness and femininity comes from an analysis of one of the other questions we asked our sampling of women: What are a woman's chief characteristics?

Again, though there is a good deal of overlapping, the answers sort out with some consistency, according to age. An interesting point here is the awakening sense of woman's liberation among the younger group, those under thirty. Here, in an almost challenging way, many women insist that there are no specific female characteristics. *There is the ability to give birth, and except for the different genitalia that is all!* But others, even some of those under twenty, list *thoughtfulness, flirtatiousness, giggling,* while some think in terms of relationships. *Willing to give up a bit of herself. Taking care of others. Making a man feel comfortable and secure. Being loving and soft to others.*

The next group, thirty to forty-five, begin to settle for a slightly different view of the same characteristics in the making of a woman. *Understanding. Courage. The ability to nurture. Quiet watchfulness. Emotion with logic. Intelligence. Righteousness. Self-pity. Generosity.*

There is an air of saintliness that begins to creep into the way women see themselves in marked contrast to the way men see them. There is always in this type of accounting, the question of what colors the view of the viewer. Are women seeing themselves as they honestly believe they are, or as society has conditioned them to see women? When they list a series of female characteristics, are the characteristics all qualities they see and sense in other women, or are they ideal qualities they would like to see in themselves?

Women over forty-five see themselves dependent on men, and yet without any contradiction they know that they take care of men. These women see themselves as *perceptive, cautious* and all of them drift toward the intellectual qualities. *Emotionally logical. Able to see through a situation. Sticking to the point. Well-balanced.*

It is interesting and a little surprising that this view of themselves occurs at a time shortly after the menopause, that turbulent period of readjustment. It is also a time of the beginning of widowhood and in many cases the end of family involvement.

In the oldest group, there is a return to younger values. *A woman is concerned with clothes. She is always conscious of her appearance. She wants to age gracefully. She is well mannered.* Again this reflects turn-of-the-century values.

Cutting across the years, a view of woman as she sees herself is a being at once calm, intelligent, understanding, humorous, sure of herself and yet deferring to man, dependent upon men and a mother to men. She feels most womanly when she is sexually involved, at least in her younger years. Later her womanliness depends on her children's love, and then on the love of people in general.

The Feminine "Reality"

But let's look at womanliness from the point of view of a "native" of today's world. A woman who has come of age in the years since World War II. Let's go from composite case histories to a young woman writer.

Robin Morgan has just hit thirty, that magic dividing line beyond which, youth tells us, "no one can be trusted." Robin Morgan has been a leading and articulate voice in the Women's Liberation Movement. A hint of the Mad Housewife syndrome comes out in Morgan's description of today's housewife. She "is forced into a totally dependent position paying for her keep with an enormous amount of emotional and physical labor which is not even considered work."

Well, our Mad Housewife was not ground down by the physical labor of housework. Nor are many middle-class women. There are too many labor-saving devices available, from the automatic dishwasher to the "hired girl." So, with the middle-class woman it must be the "emotional labor" that is so telling, so destructive.

Morgan, in her introduction to *Sisterhood Is Powerful,* a Women's Liberation anthology, holds that our society revolves totally around its men and isolates its women. She speaks of the family as it now exists as having a paranoic possession of wife and children.

To her, as to most of the women in Women's Lib organizations, womanliness is a state of bondage, a thinly disguised slavery. All the qualities of womanliness—all the qualities that women listed in our questionnaire: calmness, intelligence, understanding, humor, deference to men—they see as great lies that have been forced upon women. Women are no calmer than men; their calm, Morgan holds, is simply that of the slave who has learned to accept her role, knowing that to forget it brings only repression. She is no more intelligent than men, she says, but for that matter she is no less intelligent. Her understanding is that of the slave. You damned well understand your master or you find yourself in trouble. And her humor—surely it's the humor of all oppressed peoples.

As for deferring to men, woman has done this for centuries. But not, Morgan believes, because it makes her comfortable or because it is a built-in biological quality. Nor is it because woman is instinctively subordinate but for one reason only—man has oppressed her. This, Morgan claims, is the true reason for woman's subordination.

From Morgan's point of view, that of the new liberation

woman, there is something wrong with every concept of womanliness that has ever been presented in our society. Woman in truth is none of these things, they say. These are all qualities that have been laid upon her by the dominant sex, by men.

If this is so, then what is a woman really? Morgan and many, if not all of her sisters in the liberation movement, would have it that outside of the physical there are no differences between men and women and even the physical ones are minor. Men and women are different because of the way they are brought up.

From the very beginning boy-children are given "masculine" toys and girl-children "feminine" toys. Boys are dressed in blue and girls are dressed in pink. Different endearments are used for each, even in the cradle, and these endearments shape their personalities differently. The boy is hardened from the start, encouraged to be aggressive, made much of when he is brave and courageous, when he is, in short, displaying all the characteristics that the society thinks of as masculine. He is punished when he is soft, afraid, tender, sentimental, when he displays any of the characteristics the society thinks of as feminine. The punishment may simply be disapproval.

The girl is conditioned toward "feminine" pursuits and ways. She is encouraged to be shy, to be cowardly, to be submissive, to play quietly in girl fashion, and she is punished if she steps into the boy's role. From the very beginning, liberation women maintain, boys and girls are taught the roles they must play and they dare not step out of these roles for fear of society. This, and this only, they claim, makes them womanly or manly.

The Endless Orgasm

Another view of womanliness suggests an incompatibility that is frightening to both men and women. This view is presented by one of the scientific spokesmen for the Women's Liberation Movement.

Dr. Mary Jane Sherfey has practiced psychiatry for over fifteen years. She is an assistant professor at Cornell Medical School and has published her theory of female sexuality in the *Journal of the American Psychoanalytic Association*.

Dr. Sherfey starts her theory with an absolutely stunning conclusion. She postulates the existence of "the universal and physically normal condition of women's inability ever to reach complete sexual satiation in the presence of the most intense, repetitive orgasmic experience, no matter how produced."

I can see James Bond turning white with horror at this statement. Translated out of psychoanalytic jargon it means that no matter how much sex a woman has with a man she still won't be satisfied. Ten minutes, half an hour, a whole day won't do it. Oh, she'll have her orgasm, and after that another and another, but they won't "satiate" her. She'll demand more and more and more. "Theoretically a woman could go on having orgasms indefinitely if physical exhaustion did not intervene," Dr. Sherfey says, and then she cites the work of Masters and Johnson, the St. Louis sex researchers, to support her statement.

There is, however, a curious disconnection between what

she cites and what she concludes. Nowhere in the work of Masters and Johnson is it suggested that the ability to have continual multiple orgasms without satiation is a characteristic of all women or even many women. Perhaps there are a few, a very few who fall into this category, but to extrapolate from these few to all women is somewhat wild.

Dr. Sherfey says, "Should these preliminary findings hold," speaking of Masters and Johnson's discovery that non-orgasmic women could be taught to have orgasms, "an almost total biologic etiology of coital frigidity will be proved." Again, to translate, since the findings are no longer preliminary and have held, almost all women are frigid. None has been able to be completely satisfied.

She adds that the magnitude of the physiological and social problems facing modern womankind is difficult to contemplate. Indeed yes, and we might ask her, have women always lied about sexual satisfaction and satiation? I know that many do, perhaps more than any of us realize. A good many gynecologists have told me that the number of women patients who confess that they fake orgasm is staggering. But this, I believe, is a function of the basic incompatibility between the sexes, not a biological or physiological function of women. Women, Masters and Johnson have proved, if they've proved anything, are all capable of reaching orgasm and being satiated.

Virginia Johnson once told me that no man should write any definitive article on the female orgasm, for no man truly understands it, but I have grave doubts that Dr. Sherfey understands it either. The nymphomania she attributes to all women simply does not exist, if women themselves are capable judges.

The writing of women on the female orgasm again and

| 75

again testifies to the fact that it is a complete entity, like the male orgasm. It does not end with ejaculation, but it does, like the male orgasm, end with satiation. Unlike the male orgasm it consists of a number of mounting cycles, each somewhat greater in strength. These can vary apparently from a few, three, four or five; to many, ten or even fifty in some few women. And inevitably, if the stimulation is continued properly, these mounting cycles culminate in one final orgasm that produces satiation.

Try any serious lovemaking with a woman after that final orgasm and you know that satiation has been reached.

Why then Dr. Sherfey's strange view of womanhood? She goes on in her article to see all women as not biologically built for the "single-spouse, monogamous marital structure." She believes, however, that up till now the survival of the human species "lay in the extended family with its private property, kinship lineages, inheritance laws, social advances and most significantly, many surviving children." But she also adds that this patriarchal system led to the "ruthless subjugation of female sexuality, this forceful suppression of women's inordinate sexual demands was a prerequisite to the dawn of every modern civilization," she explains.

She paints a picture of all women as having potentially insatiable sexual appetites. These appetites have been forced under control by male domination but they still exist, panting in the dark shadows that lie in everyone's soul. Make love to a woman at your own risk. If you are a man you may find yourself enslaved for days on end in a futile effort to satisfy that "insatiable appetite."

What a strange, strange view to come from the Women's Liberation Movement. And it does come as one of their views, for Dr. Sherfey's article has been included in *Sister-*

hood Is Powerful. It is strongly reminiscent of a dark-mirrored reflection of the Freudian view of sexuality, a view that Women's Lib itself bitterly opposes.

This concept of womanliness, as a dark lurking and insatiable appetite waiting to devour men, is one of the necessary concepts for the coming Armageddon between the sexes which, according to Women's Liberation, is inevitable. Men and women are too incompatible, they say, to exist in one civilization. Men will never give up the beachhead they have achieved, and women will never again be satisfied to take second place. Armageddon is around the corner!

5

How Women See Men

A Young Woman's Fancy

Linda is eighteen and attends a girls' college in the Midwest. Fortunately there is a "brother" college a quarter of a mile away, and both schools share the same campus and the same classes. Linda is that classic breed of "long-legged American beauty" whose cool brunette looks are so difficult to decipher. None of the boys is quite sure of what goes on behind her lovely face.

"Linda," one of them said, "is more interested in sports than boys. She never misses a swimming meet and she knows every pro football player in both leagues."

I received a slightly different version of her interest in sports from Linda herself. In a candid moment she told me, "My roommate Janie and I go down to the pool to watch the swimming meets whenever we can. I don't care about the competition, but all that yummy beef! Those chests and arms and tank suits, wow!"

What about pro football?

"When I see the quarterback fade back for a pass, and

I see his neat little ass in those tight football pants—oh wow!"

Women in our society, I have been told by psychologists, do not see men the same way men see women. To a man, a woman is a commodity, and the major part of her value is her sexual attractiveness. The woman who meets the standards of beauty set up by the society, the woman who most closely approximates Raquel Welch or Ursula Andress, is the one who attracts men.

One of the bitterest cries to come from Women's Liberation is, "Men are only attracted to pretty girls. What about the rest of us who are ugly or fat or too tall? Aren't we desirable too?" It takes one back to Gilbert and Sullivan whose battle axe, Katisha, admitted that she was "sufficiently decayed" but also announced proudly that she still had elements of beauty. "I have a left elbow that men come miles to see."

It is always the element of beauty that men look for in a woman, that poets write about, musicians sing of and artists paint. It's beauty that determines the star of any play or movie. Without it a woman is a tragic or a comic figure, an old maid or the beautiful heroine's faithful friend. She's never the one we identify with. If she gets a man, he's the comic interest.

On the other hand, to a woman, according to psychologists, a man does not represent a sex object, a commodity or a use object. If any using is to be done it will be done by him, not her. To a woman, a man represents security, a father for her children and, on a deeper level, a father for herself. He possesses the penis she could never have and always wanted. And in this respect no matter what his physical size or shape he is a satisfactory mate or lover.

We can smile sadly and weep a bit at the beautiful Romeo in Zeffirelli's *Romeo and Juliet,* but he was a young inexperienced lover. If he had lived, Romeo would probably have grown a potbelly and ended up with spindly shanks. But he would have still been an attractive husband. Why not? He was destined to become the head of the house of Montague.

We all were thrilled with the fairy-tale prince and princess, John and Jackie Kennedy in their happy-ever-after life in the castle. They both looked the part. We were surprised and indignant at the Jackie-Ari romance, but our surprise and indignation didn't last. What if he looked like the grandfather instead of the prince? He had the kingdom, the power and the glory. He was almost the richest man in the world. He didn't need youth or looks. Women just don't care about physical qualities in men.

But if this is so, why does lovely Linda lick her lips at the swimmers and get such a charge out of the quarterbacks? Ah, perhaps Linda is still too young to know the way of the world. She still dreams with Juliet and an earlier Jackie.

Is part of growing up, for a woman in our society, the renouncing of all these dreams? Must she renounce male beauty, male physical attractiveness, and accept security, wealth and power as desirable facets of maleness?"

The Roving Eye

Purpose: To help put a woman in touch with her responses to "physical" man.

The woman takes the male doll and traces it on a piece of paper, then labels the drawing HANDSOME MAN. Charting the movements of her eyes over HANDSOME MAN's body, she numbers

in order from 1 to 10 each place her
eyes stop. She then invites an older
woman to play the same game and com-
pares the results.

The Quality of Manliness

I have a good friend, a woman in her late forties, who
recently was widowed after a happy marriage. She told of
attending a singles weekend with a man she had been
"dating."

"He isn't much to look at physically, God knows. We
have fun together, but that's about all. And he hasn't any
money. At fifty he's still a bank teller. You just look at him,
and you know he's nothing. But we walked into the lounge
at this place and wham! the women descended on him as if
they were birds and he was a juicy worm. Why? I took
another long look at him and I still couldn't see what was
so special."

What was so special was the simple fact of maleness.
He was an available man, and in this age group there are
so few available men that women cannot pick and choose.
If they are to have a man at all, they must take what's available and count their blessings. There is no market for
women over thirty-five though there is a market for men
right into their sixties.

The sad fact is that by the age of forty most men of any
value are taken. "The good-looking ones go fast," my friend

told me. "And then the rich ones. Even the poor uglies get into the act. There are just too many single women available at any age, and over forty their ranks are swelled by widows and divorcees. The widowed man goes first. He has proven himself a good risk. Even the divorced man is snapped up. We all know we can do better than the dope who let him go. You know, we're so desperate that we even find ourselves taking chances with the chronic bachelors. I can change him. So he's a little gay, what's so bad about that?"

Why are there so many more women than men in this older age group? World War II started the present shortage and widows, of course, swell the ranks. Men begin to die off in their late forties leaving wives some five years younger. If women didn't marry by this age it was usually because they weren't chosen. Men who never married were not the marrying kind for one reason or another. A man divorced at forty looks around for anyone from twenty to thirty. He rarely looks beyond that age. Why should he? Why settle for older merchandise when the younger stuff is still available? A woman divorced at forty is usually just stuck. And so it goes.

The quality of manliness is rarely a physical thing for women in this age group, the late forties and fifties. They take what they can get, as long as it wears pants. And sometimes if they have to they'll even wear the pants themselves.

But even those women in this age group who are married see little of the physical as a source of attraction in their men. Basically manliness is being a good provider.

The Positive View

Let's return to the questionnaire and consider the answers of those women ranging in age from about forty-five to fifty-five. Some of them, a little over half, were working women. About 20 percent were widowed or divorced and the rest were housewives and mothers. What, in their opinion, made a man manly?

Many of them, it must be understood, felt that most of the men they encountered, including their own lovers, friends or husbands, were lacking in manliness. This would indicate that these qualities they named were ideal qualities, qualities they would like to see in their men or qualities they saw in those men they found manly.

The largest group of these women, though not most—29 percent—saw manliness as *the ability to function as a strong human being, to bear life's burden without whimpering.* A manly man was not necessarily one who came out on top of the heap. He was not the highest wage earner or the man who licked the system, but the man who stood up to the system and didn't let it grind him down. He was also the man who could be leaned on by the rest of the family in times of trouble. Strong, not in terms of physical qualities, but in his personality, in his character, in his ability to handle problems.

And is this view so very far from that authoritarian attitude of Freud and Nietzsche that reflected all the Victorian clichés? The women themselves see men as the father figure bearing the weight of the family on his shoulders and not wincing one bit. This to them is manliness.

But it isn't surprising that this should be the way this group of women sees manliness. After all, they were children in the late twenties and early thirties. Their ideals were formed in those years. And while there was a strong undercurrent of feminism, it didn't reach into most families in America. In most families of that period the old values, the trailing remnants of Victorianism, still held true.

Let's look at some of the other aspects of manliness, as seen by these women. The next largest group, 24 percent of them, thought that a man was manly when he was involved with women. And 19 percent saw a zest for life or virility as part of the manliness.

Only 9 percent of these women listed physical characteristics—*handsome, good looks, a masculine build, physical strength*—as any indication of manliness. Ten percent saw a man's relationship to children indicative of his manliness, and 9 percent saw manliness in terms of egocentric qualities. *When a man is tied up with himself, concerned about his own health, his own looks, his own feelings, then I think of him as manly. A manly man is a self-centered man.*

These were the only negative views of manliness in this group. However, when women were asked about the qualities that make a man—"male characteristics"—we got an entirely different slant from them. Over half of them listed some sort of physical strength as a male characteristic. Some tied it to athletics, and some tied it to hard work such as digging ditches or hauling wood, "hard, dirty, sweaty work."

Creativity, sensitivity, generosity, idealism were held to be male characteristics by only 3 percent of the women.

| 85

Twice that number saw men as *self-deceiving, arrogant, rigid* and *aggressive.* The rest varied in their views from *naive* to *realistic,* from *competitive* to *selfish.*

Are Men Beautiful?

What is curious is that so many women saw physical strength as a chief characteristic of men but did not believe that it made a man manly.

Yukio Mishima, the controversial Japanese novelist, in his book *Kinjiki,* declares that women have no opinions about male beauty: "Insensitive almost to the point of being blind they have a discerning eye for male beauty not greatly different from that of a normal male." He goes on to say that sensitivity to the peculiar beauties of the male is the exclusive property of the homosexual: "Women are incapable of according to the male such fleshy praise."

There is in this, as our questionnaire shows, a germ of truth. But it might be truer to say that the older a woman gets, the less likely she is to accord to the male such fleshy praise.

I recently stood in the hall of Greek statuary in New York's Metropolitan Museum of Art and watched the reaction of men and women, boys and girls to some of the more perfect male nudes. Women over forty, for the most part, accorded the statues a casual glance. Men of this age more often lingered, caressing the statues with their eyes, some even reaching out against the guard's frowns to touch them. But ah, let a younger girl come along and her eyes lit up, her lips parted and I could really see appreciation.

It reminded me in many ways of Linda's visits to the swimming meets and how she looked when she described the shoulders and chests of the swimmers. Her eyes glowed in the same way and she even surreptitiously licked her lips with her tongue. Nor was Janie, Linda's roommate, any less entranced. It leads to an obvious conclusion. When a woman is young she appreciates male beauty, male physical strength even as men appreciate women's beauty. Something happens to a woman in our society as she gets older. She loses the ability to appreciate the physical sexuality of men.

She develops instead an ability to see them as financial-sexual or good-provider-sexual. She gives up her physical needs for her social needs, for this loss of judgment is a cover-up, a psychological turnabout. Perhaps she even convinces herself that she means it and it may be in that strange way we have of believing our psychological camouflage that she does mean it. But we know that her conviction is really a mask.

Kinsey found that a woman's sexuality grows and develops after adolescence and reaches its peak in the thirties. The Mrs. Robinson syndrome begins. Logically she should become more and more aware of men's physical attraction, more and more conscious of a well-proportioned body, an athletic walk, a handsome face. And in one sense most women still are aware of all these things although they have given up such attractions in their own lives.

They settle for Harry with a bulging stomach, George without a muscle on his skinny body or Bill with his funny-looking face. But they preserve their dream life, their fantasy world. They sigh over movie stars and television personalities. They even have their favorite radio disc jockeys with "sexy" voices. Why, if they are truly no longer attracted to the physical aspects of men, do they still moon over these fantasy men?

The answer is that they still are attracted. They still feel the physical-chemical attraction of a handsome man, a sexy voice, a good-looking body. But they have buried this feeling for convenience's sake. After all, they are the underdogs in our society and they must play the game the way the rules are written, and men have written the rules.

So Myrna puts her dreams and fancies aside and turns down Bill the lifeguard with no future at all for Allen the salesman who may have a very funny build indeed, but does have a good job with a good future.

What does this make women? Men, who have set the rules, say that it makes them prostitutes—"All they want is a meal ticket."

But in truth, when the initial glow of security wears off and the frustration of life sets in, it often makes for a basic incompatibility between the sexes. Somehow the woman comes to feel that she has sold her birthright and the right to a sexual esthetic, among other things, for an economic mess of lentils. This is one of the key points of man-woman incompatibility.

The Man Haters

But let's take another look at the questionnaire. While a large percentage of younger women found physical qualities a solid part of manliness, the rest found manliness linked to the ability to be decisive, to sincerity, to strength, to love of life, aggressiveness and sensitivity, while only 3 percent held negative feelings about manliness. These few women listed man's chief characteristic as insensitivity, a defensive nature and selfishness.

There is a strong agreement between this questionnaire and a recent Harris poll of 3,000 women in America which said that 67 percent of the women polled viewed men as "kind, gentle and thoughtful."

Such a high percentage of positive feelings in women's consideration of men seems remarkable. Equally remarkable is the low negative opinion in our questionnaire of young women, particularly when you consider that most of the Women's Liberation group would be in the younger age brackets.

There was a good sprinkling of almost defiant answers that refused to see any difference between men and women, women who saw manliness as the same quality as womanliness and found men's characteristics no different from women's characteristics. But even this is a completely different view of manliness than the one I expected to find in liberation women.

Perhaps I had looked for the bitterness and venom of a Valerie Solanas whose first claim to fame was an attempt to shoot Andy Warhol and whose second was SCUM, the Society for Cutting Up Men. Of man, Solanas writes: "He is a half-dead unresponsive lunk, incapable of giving or receiving happiness; consequently he is at best an utter bore, an inoffensive blah, since only those capable of absorption in others can be charming . . . he is capable of a large array of negative feelings—hate, jealousy, contempt, disgust, guilt, shame, doubt—and moreover he is aware of what he is." (The three dots leave out much more of the same.)

A more temperate view was expressed by Germaine Greer, the Australian author, who sees men as "not so much the enemy as other kinds of slaves in bondage to unreasonable social demands." Miss Greer, who is just past the generational dividing line, thirty-two years old, makes a strong case for female sexuality and a meeting of men and women on sexual grounds.

This circles back to the way the younger women in our group saw men—rarely as the enemy, almost never with the violence of a Valerie Solanas, but perhaps in a physical light through the rosy haze of their own dawning sexuality. They search for physical qualities in their concepts of masculinity, and later, in their late twenties, they see man as manly when he relates to women, making love, being sensitive to a woman's needs, treating a woman as someone special.

Is this a reflection of society's stand that men are superior and therefore must be the active force, must be the wage earners, must exploit women and use them? I don't think so. I think this is instead a reflection of a cleaner, sounder relationship between the sexes, a basic compatibility that can exist and eventually, when we have become fully civilized, will and must exist. Today, as has been the case throughout recorded time, men and women are incompatible. For untold centuries they managed this incompatibility because man had the upper hand and women were the oppressed "second sex." Now any successful oppression needs the cooperation of the oppressed person. He or she must be firmly convinced of the psychological validity of that oppression. Women have, as far back as myth and legend and even farther, probably into paleolithic times, been psychologically convinced of their own physical and mental inferiority.

The Good Old Days

With the awakening realization of woman's oppression, there has also come the growing awareness of the incompatibility between the sexes. The knowledge of this incompatibility has made not only women dissatisfied with their lot, with the man-woman situation in our culture, but it has also made men dissatisfied. Men are now looking back with wistful eyes at the "solid" virtues of our father's fathers, saying, "There was a time! The *family* existed then, and there were the good values of good relationships. The father worked, often with his hands, and the sweat of his labor was good. The mother worked too, and produced a home she was proud of. The children knew the meanings of good and bad. What has happened? What has gone wrong?"

In truth, nothing has gone wrong. The "solid" virtues of our fathers are all fantasies we have created. There has never been a period in recorded history that really corresponded to the fantasy world men always build up around their parents' childhood. What men miss is not the innocence of childhood, but the security of having had the upper hand for so long.

The incompatibility of men and women is now out in the open and men's security is shattered, but only until he can pick up the pieces and remold them in a more honest shape. Once men and women face up to their incompatibility, they can begin to enjoy it.

Vive la Difference

Purpose: To force the man and woman to come to grips with the qualities they feel embody "manliness" and "womanliness." The differences in their responses will offer the key to their incompatibility.

Each partner takes a male doll and rapidly "tattoos" him with 10 characteristics that make a man manly.

Each then takes a female doll and rapidly "tattoos" her with 10 characteristics that make a woman womanly.

Neither should let the other see his "tattoos" until they are both ready to compare and discuss them.

6

The Predator With a Brain: How Men See Themselves

Obscene But Not Illegal

Over 75 percent of all the men we polled, regardless of age, listed physical strength as a necessary attribute of manliness. Only a small percentage of the women agreed, and these were younger women.

A psychologist once told me that men see other men through the eyes of women. I think it's more likely that they see other men as they believe women see them. Men have a firm conviction that women are impressed with male strength, with male genitals, with all the physical aspects of maleness.

I was walking with an Italian-American friend recently and we passed a group of construction workers taking a noon break. There were about ten of them lounging in the shade, whistling at the girls who walked past and trying, with either an off-key whistle or an intimate phrase, to throw the girls off balance. One young worker with black hair and bright eyes would walk toward the oncoming girls, catch their eye, then grab his own genitals.

I stopped in surprise and my friend asked, "What's the matter?"

"Did you see what I saw? Did he grab himself where I thought he did? He practically waved the damn thing at her!"

"Oh!" my friend laughed. "He's a paisan, an Italian. Besides he kept his fly zipped. He may have been obscene, but he wasn't illegal."

As we walked on I said, "How do you know he was Italian?"

"He looked Italian, and besides, it's an old Italian peasant gesture, grabbing yourself there. Supposed to bowl the girls over."

I thought he was joking, but then in a recent realistic Italian movie I saw the same overt gesture made by a worker as a pretty girl walked past him.

In both cases the gesture had no effect on the girl except a negative one. And yet I'm sure that the fact that it didn't work, or perhaps never works, doesn't stop it from being used. It's a little like the old joke of the two men walking down the street. Each time they pass a girl, one of them stops her and says, "Can I screw you?"

Each girl slaps his face and walks on indignantly. Finally his friend asks him, "Do you say that to every girl? Do you ask every girl you meet if she'll screw you?"

"Every girl!"

"Boy, you must get slapped a lot."

"Sure, but I get screwed a lot too."

The body-language gesture, on the other hand, grabbing the genitals, probably never gets results, and yet it is still repeated, not only in the Italian working-class culture, but, as I have since found out, all over the world. The general feeling among men seems to be that faced with irrefutable evidence of a man's masculinity a woman will succumb. That the theory has no validity doesn't seem to matter. It is still accepted. It is not something, incidentally, restricted to working-class people. There are middle-class and intellectual variations on it. It is certainly reflected in the current pornography explosion. There are literally dozens of pornographic novels now on sale in almost every bookstore, and there is hardly one that does not have some scene in which the hero, by simply exposing his "magnificent organ, erect and quivering," reduces the girl to quiescent jelly.

On the literary side, one of the main themes in Ernest Hemingway's writings was a concern for the evidence of masculinity and the conviction that once produced it would be irresistible to women.

Men inevitably believe that women are concerned with the "manly" elements of man—and this belief is a reflection of their own concern with such elements. From childhood on men feel in competition with other men about the size of their genitals. Their fantasies revolve around the conviction that women too share this concern, though study after study indicates that they don't.

But it is not only the physical aspects of maleness that concern men, the genitals, the muscles, body size and strength. It is also the psychological aspects of maleness as they are seen on our society, courage, aggressiveness, dominance, ruthlessness.

A careful reading of Hemingway's work makes you

realize that he was even more concerned with the reaction of other men to his masculinity than with women's reaction.

There is nothing necessarily homosexual in this concern. Nor is there anything unusual. Scratch the surface of most men and you will find that often their happiest days were spent in the company of other men.

The Happiest Days of Our Lives

I had dinner recently in a strange city with a contemporary of mine. We had met in a business way, and we had worked together during the day. At dinner we faced each other alone for the first time, and both of us knew a moment of panic as we reached desperately through our experiences for some common ground of conversation. We wanted to avoid business, and politics was too risky for we had to work together the next day.

I mentioned the war and his face lit up. "I was in the Pacific during World War II," he began. And I sat back, knowing the problem was solved.

For two hours we talked of his war experiences, not the actual combat, for he had seen very little of that, but tales of the outfit he was in and his wild experiences. There was the time he had been drunk on a coral atoll while his plane took off with all his orders, the day he and his buddies had been left to guard his company's beer ration, the girl he had been half in love with in Fiji . . . the stories went on and on.

Halfway through them I found myself bemused by his preoccupation with those days. They had only lasted eighteen months and they had occurred thirty years ago. But for him they were the high point, the most exciting part of his life. They were the years he had spent in the company of other men.

What is there about the company of men that is so exciting to other men? What is so important, so true? Most men who have gone to all-boys schools or all-boys camps will remember them as "good old days." I spent my summers at an all-boys camp over thirty years ago, and even today when I meet someone from those days there is an instant rapport, a remembering when. How strange that so brief a time can be stronger in emotional intensity than all the years since. And yet not so strange if we consider just that emotional intensity.

I remember very vividly the one summer in camp when I was elected to the camp's select secret society. In those days summer camps were not progressive in any way. Competition was the name of the game and the idea of a secret society that selected only five or six campers each year was not as terrible as we think it is today.

I had attended the same camp summer after summer since I was eight, but it was not until I was fifteen years old that I finally made the secret society. I cannot recall the society's name now, but I do very clearly recall the initiation ceremony. The five of us who were selected were blindfolded and led from one humiliation to another for the better part of an entire summer night.

We were paddled frequently along the way. The sole point of the initiation was to break down our resistance, to frighten us or to get us to cry. For our part we knew that to get through the initiation we would have to grit our teeth and act impassive. In the concluding part of the initiation we were each led to an isolated spot on a mountain where we were told to wait in silent vigil until we were collected. We were not collected until noon of the next day.

Rites of Passage

In some ways that vigil, for all of the boys on manhood's edge, was a deeply moving experience. We came out of it tried and found to measure up. We were men and welcomed to the company of men personified by the secret society whose members had all proven to be courageous and loyal. We were forbidden then to speak to any non-member about the initiation and this drew us even closer to each other. We were a select group, a very special group.

The feeling of selection, of being one with a group against the world, was tremendously important to us at the ages of fourteen, fifteen or sixteen. It gave us a sense of strength that few of us could achieve alone. There was in this very special group an almost mystical power that each group member could draw upon. It was also a situation peculiarly masculine.

Some behavioral scientists wonder if there is a mechanism that operates to produce a biological basis for secret societies, fraternities, clubs and so on. They stress the fact that these societies are predominantly male. They point out that in primitive societies the passage from childhood to adulthood is marked by secret initiations. In our more sophisticated societies the initiations into all male groups often seem pale copies of these primitive rites of passage.

Sororities may have their secret initiations but from the stories I have heard from many college girls their rites are far less meaningful than those of men, and are simply a necessary device for entering a group where special privilege becomes the dominant attraction.

Among men, however, the initiation rite itself is a "moment of truth." It usually contains a special mystical significance. If in the company of other men we can pass these trials and tests that separate the brave from the cowardly, then we are also capable of passing from childhood to manhood.

Lionel Tiger attributes this need for passage and proving oneself, for a physical trial of our masculinity, to some dark time of conflict with women in our prehistoric past. Envying women the ability to give birth, perhaps the one function he could not take away from her, primitive man attempted his own act of birth from childhood to manhood, a rite of passage that imitated his first birth into the world, but this time he did it without women. The initiation ceremony accompanying this symbolic birth consisted of secrets supposedly stolen from women in the distant past, secrets presumably of how to give birth.

There may be some truth in this as there is possibly truth in Tiger's contention that the urge to form secret societies is a part of man's built-in urge to form groups in general, an urge that comes down to us from our hunting forebears who had to operate in groups to ensure their own survival.

| 99

Winner Take All

Purpose: To help the man experience successful competition with another man.

The man takes a male doll and calls it ME, then selects a second male doll and calls it OPPONENT.

He chooses the area of their competition from the following: politics, business, personal life, love, athletics, etc.

Using any assault tactic that occurs to him, he must defeat his opponent.

To me it seems that the secret society initiation is often more important than the society and itself may satisfy a basic need in man. As a child moving into a slum neighborhood, I had to face initiation into the local street gang. Initiation consisted of fighting each gang member in turn from the weakest to the strongest. Somewhere along the line exhaustion, plus the superior strength of my opponent at the moment, decided the fight. From that day on my status in the gang was determined by how many boys I had beaten and who had beaten me. To gain any further status I had, in some subtle way, to initiate a fight with the boy who had beaten me. If I lost I stayed at the same level. If I won I stepped up a level, and could then consider the next boy in line and decide whether to fight him.

The gang itself functioned only spasmodically, but the initiation rite was very rigidly held, whether the newcomer wanted to join or not. Lest this be thought only a function of childhood, I ran into very much the same situation in the army as a young man. In training, our barracks was run by a very rigid status line, and you only crossed the line by physically beating the man ahead of you. My "moment of truth" came when I had a fist fight with a sergeant in the "old army." I won because of an excess of Adrenalin and size, and I came out of the fight with no desire to ever talk to my opponent again. I didn't like fighting, and I didn't like being forced into the fight.

To my amazement the sergeant considered me, as he put it "an asshole buddy." Nothing would do but that the two of us go out drinking together that night. To him the fight was my initiation, no more and no less. It was a rite of passage for me and, once over, should be completely forgotten. I had proved myself in his eyes, and I could take my place alongside him.

Flirting With Fear

The term he used, which I heard continuously in the army, "asshole buddy," is based, of course, on a homosexual joke, and it is just that, a joke. Yet it is very strange that this should be funny to men, that homosexuality should be at once abnormal among most men—and it is—and yet have such a compulsive attraction. Men who apparently have no homosexuality in their makeup will continually flirt with the idea, tease each other about it, mimic homosexual ways and inevitably find some way of working homosexuality into initiation ceremonies.

Tiger describes a fraternity initiation in which the candidates (stripped nude, were given Vaseline and a nail. They were told to grease the nail and to form a circle exposing their buttocks and were handed the greased nail. The initiation was then ended by the candidate being whacked on the buttocks. The symbolism of the greased nail, the anticipation of it being driven into the rectum, the open buttocks, are all a terrifying flirtation with homosexuality.

This same flirtation occurred during the summer camp secret society initiation I described earlier. At one point, stripped naked, we were told to manipulate our penises. We were blindfolded and nude in a secluded spot. The impossibility of attaining an erection was obvious, yet the group conducting the initiation proceeded to humiliate us for our shrunken penises and our lack of manhood. The high point of the incident was an egg broken over our genitals. Blindfolded we only had the sensation of moisture and mess. We were then beaten and paddled for losing control of ourselves.

The paddling, too, so much a part of all male initiations that in college fraternities the paddles used are made by the initiates as "labors of love," has a homosexual-cum-sado-masochistic connotation.

Why this repulsion and attraction to homosexuality among men? There seems to me no complementary attitude among women. They never seem to have the same involvement with lesbianism that men have with male homosexuality. And while there are literally dozens of jokes that men tell involving homosexuals there are few, if any, that women tell involving lesbians. Nor have I ever seen a woman imitate a lesbian for laughs.

A man's involvement with homosexuality symbolizes many things, not the least of which is an uncertainty about his own masculinity. Our society with all its heavy emphasis on masculinity has laid down very rigid rules for a man. These rules all involve acting in what the society considers "a manly way." We have seen from the questionnaire that this manliness consists in part of physical strength and a sexual involvement with women. Another aspect of the same manliness is our relationship with other men.

In this society strict proscription prevent us from physical shows of affection between two men. We are not allowed to kiss other men or to hold hands with other men. In some of us, any sort of physical contact with another man arouses anxiety. And yet, although we are repelled by the physical contact of homosexuality, we are also attracted by it. We flirt with it for the same reason we flirt with death. We do not want to die on a conscious level, but many of us want to experience the thrill of the near-death or the missed-death. Karl Menninger believes that men have proportionately more of this death wish, or of the tendency to destroy themselves, than women have. We climb mountains for the risks involved, enjoying it all the more if one false step means disaster. We race cars and ride rapids and sky dive and the closer to destruction we get, the keener the excitement.

We achieve manhood and manliness and the ultimate in masculinity if we can flirt with death on a realistic level knowing that the slightest slip may kill us. For this reason the most masculine professions are the most dangerous—a policeman, a fireman, a test pilot, an auto racer, an astronaut, a deep-sea diver, a football player, a bullfighter, a construction worker.

We can also assert our masculinity by second-hand participation in danger, by watching a football game, by reading about dangerous sports and professions, even by watching steelmakers raising a building. Our flirtation with death is less intense for being once removed but it is still there. Perhaps the violence reflected in the current spate of television reflects some of this. Mannix, Dragnet, Mission Impossible, Dan August are all heavy with violence and are all male favorites.

We assert our masculinity by flirting with death and in a similar way we assert it by flirting with homosexuality. Each joke we tell about a faggot, a fruit or a queen secures our own place in the world of the truly masculine. We cannot really appreciate that place unless we see it by contrast with those men who have sacrificed masculinity as we know it and have chosen the "gay" world.

If we flirt with that world and yet renounce it, we are all the stronger for the renunciation.

It is a form of "testing," one of the most basic and primitive magics, so much a part of our heritage that it may well have a biological base in our nature. We use testing magic even in our dreams. We dream of the most terrible tragedies, of the deaths of ourselves or our loved ones only to "test out" such incidents, to see if we can survive their happening. In the same way we use the magic of testing in our flirtation with homosexuality.

A Predatory Squid

Tiger, in his work, has made a strong case for male bonding, the need of men for the company of other men. Perhaps it is the safety in numbers which makes the testing bearable. Male bonding is not at all a new concept. Writers have always recognized it with varying degrees of joy or sadness. It is the quality behind the nights out with the boys, the male drinking parties and hunting parties, the fact that in almost any culture when a party starts the men drift together to talk "man talk."

Tiger sees male bonding related to the persistence of the hunting instinct, but the hunting instinct has persisted in other ways, and I'd like to consider one of them.

Man is and always has been a predatory animal, and his predatory drive has survived into our present civilization. It is strongest in the male of our species, though to some degree in the female as well. The old line that the female of the species is more deadly than the male applies only occasionally to homo sapiens. In the vast majority of instances, the male of homo sapiens had been proved more deadly, and the predatory drive more active in him.

I do not hold that this predatory drive is entirely bad. Consider the case of the squid. For eons, in the early Paleozoic era, mollusks developed slowly, leisurely and defensively. They clung to rocks with their bivalve shells undulating the water through their gills and stomachs, and they were content to digest any unhappy sea life that wandered in.

But not the remote ancestor of the squid. For some peculiar reason, associated with the movement of evolution's irresistible tide, the proto-squid became restless at clinging to rocks and waiting for his food to come to him. Instead he took off after his prey and turned into a predator. Over the generations his shell shrank to a vestigial bit of skeleton, and the tentacles he used to grasp his prey became larger and more flexible. He developed eyes and, most important of all, a rudimentary brain, and with it the dawning of intelligence.

How far the squid rose up the evolutionary ladder is

debatable, but if we measure his progress against his distant evolutionary cousins, the clams and mussels, we can see a fantastic difference in intelligence, whatever that is.

The development of intelligence is always a spin-off of the predatory way of life, and I believe it was man's choice of predatory ways that initially developed his brain and reasoning power. It is very likely that man originally evolved as a pack-hunting carnivore.

What happened to man was that eventually the brain and reasoning power made his predatory nature unnecessary. He no longer had to stalk and hunt. As civilization developed, he obtained sufficient control of his environment to domesticate his own prey.

When this happened the biologically built-in need to be a predator took other paths. Robert Ardrey, in his book *The Territorial Imperative,* considered man's territorial needs and attempted to link them to an aggressive need for war. "The principal cause of modern warfare arises from the failure of an intruding power correctly to estimate the defensive resources of a territorial defender," Ardrey said, but it seems to me that this is a naive interpretation of the forces behind war. It may, however, be one of the reasons why seemingly sensible men can often be rallied to die for a senseless cause.

Instincts and Drives

Man's predatory past may be one of the reasons he can be involved in war, but it seems more logical to search for the predatory instinct in other aspects of his life, in areas where he is not forced to participate. We can look for remnants of the predatory instinct in competitive sports. We can also find very obvious traces of it in the many and various ways that man, within his cultural framework, preys on his fellow men.

Certainly the desire to dominate other men in business and politics is a logical reflection of our predatory past, and the tendency of men to use other men as well as women seems a direct reflection of predation. Heterosexual men will even exploit other men sexually in certain situations.

I was told by a young man who had been sent to a city prison that he was forced to undergo two degrading initiations: one was by the prison guards who used him sexually, and a second by the prisoners who raped him one by one, starting with the strongest and working down to the weakest. This is no isolated or unusual case. The forced homosexuality of all prisons is well known and has been well documented.

In one sense, then, we can look at homosexuality as well as heterosexuality as a working out of our predatory drives. I use the word drives, rather than instincts, because I do not believe there are many real instincts left in humans. If there are (the sucking instinct in a newborn baby may be one) they are soon outgrown. We have come into a state of humanness trailing remnants of instincts watered down, in the human condition, to drives.

The great dividing line between men and animals is in this loss of instinct. We no longer have an instinct for sexual intercourse, an instinct to satisfy hunger, an instinct to stake out our territory by leaving spoor, an instinct to attack any male of our own species.

Instead we have urges or drives. We are driven toward sex, toward satisfying our hunger, to being aggressive under certain circumstances and, if Tiger is correct, we are driven toward male bonding. The fact that these are only drives becomes obvious if we consider the difference between instinctive and learned behavior. As an example, wasps build nests instinctively. In fact, if a wasp builds half a nest and half of that is destroyed he will continue to build the remaining half on the undestroyed first part. It doesn't matter if the finished mess is inadequate. He is performing an instinctive act.

A man builds a house after learning how. If half of what he has built is destroyed he will either modify the rest of the house or first repair the destroyed part and then build the rest. In both the wasp and man there may be a drive to build. The wasp satisfies the drive by instinct, the man by learned behavior.

There are species of ants that enslave other ants by instinct. Humans enslave other humans because of a predatory drive to use them and an intellectual rationalization of that drive.

Sexual union in the human has become a drive, not an instinct, so much so that we must learn how to perform the act. There are vestigial and instinctive remnants connected with it, such as the male pelvic thrusting, but in general the act must be learned. There are recorded cases, so many that they are not even considered rare, of marriages that have lasted for years without sexual union taking place between the husband and wife. For one reason or another they couldn't learn how, and shame, embarrassment or guilt prevented them from finding out. The recent Masters and Johnson study of sexual problems indicated just how widespread sexual difficulties of this kind are. If sex were an instinct these difficulties would not occur.

The drive toward sex is probably stronger than any other human drive, except perhaps the drive to satisfy hunger. Yet strong as it is, we are able to control it, to modify it, to sublimate it. We have been able to deny it completely and remain celibate. If we can thus control this strongest of all drives, it follows that we can also control the weaker drives, those toward predation and aggression, toward power and the control of other humans and the drive to use other people.

We can also control the drive in men to use women, and with this control achieve a compatibility between men and women. But more of this later.

Who Is in the Driver's Seat?

The problem then centers around control of our drives. Can we control them or do they control us? In the fascinating novel by William Golding, *Lord of the Flies*, we are shown just how close to the surface these slumbering drives lie. *Lord of the Flies* deals with a group of English schoolboys wrecked on a deserted island during World War II. There is adequate food but no controls and the children revert to savagery, only a few holding out for order and these are either killed or defeated.

The novel, according to Lionel Tiger, is concerned with "Species-specific patterns . . . coalition, aggression, violence, and the savor of blood." We might argue that *Lord of the Flies* is just a novel and at best only one man's view of the basic savagery beneath the surface of man and boys.

But a very disturbing fact emerged when *Lord of the Flies* was made into a motion picture. The film was done on an island similar to the one in the novel, and the boy actors were organized to duplicate the conditions of the book.

The director, Peter Brook, in an article about the boys and the filming wrote, "Many of their off-screen relationships completely paralleled the story, and one of our main problems was to encourage them to be uninhibited within the shots but disciplined in between."

He goes on to tell how relationships between the boys broke down, how some of them even terrified the actor playing the part of Piggy, the loyal but physically unfortunate fat boy. They convinced him that he would have a rock dropped on him toward the end of the filming, and he would be killed for the camera.

"My experience showed me," Brook said, "that the only falsification to Golding's fable is the length of time that savagery takes. I believe that if the cork of continued adult presence were removed from the bottle the complete catastrophe could occur within a long week-end."

Alas, what a blow for man's rise from savagery.

7

It's Tough to Be a Man

Gross Skills and Fine Skills

"The trouble between the sexes starts at an alarmingly early age," a psychologist friend of mine told me. "From the very beginning there is a difference in development. Boys and girls mature at different rates and in different directions. The boys achieve gross motor strength first while the girls achieve fine motor skills. This, when you come down to it, is the basic difference between boys and girls. Boys learn to rough and tumble. Girls as a rule play in a more delicate way. The boys are just not ready to use fine skills at as early an age as the girls are."

Gross motor skills, my friend explained to me, are those skills involving running, jumping, shouting, the untrammeled actions of childhood, whereas fine motor skills are the skills that allow careful discrimination, work with the fingers, sewing, printing, writing. He pointed out that in elementary school if a teacher shouts, "Sit down, stop fidgeting, stop running," she is always shouting at a boy. When a boy bothers a girl, he pulls her hair and punches her. When a girl bothers a boy she uses her "fine motor control" to pinch him.

The boy and girl enter school at the same age, but the school system favors the girl for it is predicated on the use of fine motor skills, the girl's strongest point. There is very little chance in elementary school for the boy to act out his gross motor needs. He can only run and jump and be athletic in gym or at recess, and even then he's toned down. During the school day there is almost no physical activity available, certainly very little gross motor activity. The boy must learn to hold a pencil and practice penmanship and in general be forced into a development of fine motor skills to compete with the girls on their terms, a competition he is just not capable of handling.

This is where the imbalance starts, but it need not be this way at all. Teaching in elementary schools could be changed to take advantage of the boys' different development. Boys could learn to use their strength in gross motor activity to solve problems. How? Well, as one simple example, math, traditionally an exercise in fine motor skills, could be slanted to take advantage of gross motor behavior. Distance and time could be measured by clocking how long it takes a boy to walk a certain distance. He would thus be using his body, using his strength, using his activity to learn mathematical facts. A little thought will make it obvious how easy it is to apply this type of physical problem-solving to all learning.

It's a Woman's World

Unfortunately, most teachers of very young children are women. Until very recently all were women, but now a few men are beginning to break into the field. But the wages are still too low and the job is unattractive to men with families. Our teaching system is therefore oriented toward girls and run by women. They have neither the time nor the inclination and training to use methods that would exploit the boys' skills. As a result the typical boy begins to develop into a man in a female world, female at school and hardly less female at home. There is a father but most of the time he's no more in evidence than the male principal of the school to which the boy goes.

Traditionally, the mother runs the home and does most toward rearing the children, boys as well as girls. The father is away all day, and when he returns in the evening he is often more concerned with his own relaxation than with the identity of his son.

What happens to boys raised in a world of women? Sometimes they do well, but in many cases they come to identify too closely with women. They may be unsure of their own masculinity or even turn into homosexuals in a strange love-hate relationship that sees woman's love as betrayal. Even when they grow up "straight" women are always sources of trouble.

Lederer, in an analysis of *Grimm's Fairy Tales*, comes up with an interesting tabulation of women that reflects how most men view them. In two hundred tales, he found wicked mothers or step-mothers in sixteen but wicked fathers or step-fathers in only three. There were twenty-three wicked female witches and only two wicked male witches. Treacherous maids who killed or endangered their suitors numbered thirteen but there was only one evil male who harmed his bride. There were nine bad sisters to one bad brother.

This is the stuff childhood fantasies are made of, and none of it augurs well for the young man starting out in life. He knows what to expect from women. They will play the heavy in his adult life. Even if this knowledge of a woman's perfidy is subconscious, it is still there. He learns that ultimately women will use and exploit him.

Ah, but isn't it the other way around? Aren't men the predators, the exploiters, the users of women? Isn't this what Women's Liberation is all about?

True, they are, and it is. But nothing is simple in our complex society. Things are seldom all black or all white, but there is instead a vast intermingling of grays. The exploited class develops its own techniques of exploitation, and women, traditionally downtrodden, have learned to use men. Take the case of John and Charlotte.

The Case of John and Charlotte

From John's viewpoint: "When I married Charlotte everything was roses and honeysuckle. We were both working and Charlotte didn't want to give up her job. I didn't think she should either. She was assistant buyer at Altman's department store, and it paid well and she liked the work. But we put her salary into a separate bank account. Why hers? Well, that was her idea. After all, she pointed out, I was the man in the family, and she was right, of course. She was pregnant within a year, and that extra money went fast. With our second kid things got rough. Charlotte decided she didn't want to go back to work. What the hell, a kid needs a mother."

Charlotte became a full-time housewife and mother. "I wasn't too happy about it," John said. "Mainly I had the feeling that Charlotte was working too hard at it. She was alone in the apartment with the kids all day. We have a small place, and it doesn't take that much cleaning. We've got a washing machine and a dryer in the bathroom, so what's the big deal. What I mean is, every night Charlotte was pooped, and she'd snipe at me making it very clear that I was responsible. All of a sudden they became *my* kids. It was *my* house, and she had given up *her* career for me.

"I began to get a boxed-in feeling. Hell, it wasn't for me she had stopped work. We had talked it all over and *she* didn't want her kids raised by a housekeeper. *She* wanted to be a mother, to take care of the house and kids. I didn't force her into that. For that matter, what did I get out of it? I break my balls at the office, and still I can't keep up with the payments on the apartment, the car, the washing machine, I'm looking for a job at night. The only answer is some moonlighting, but Charlotte gets all sullen when I suggest it, Christ, I just want her off my back. I want to get out of the house. I can't face the unspoken accusations that are part of every talk we have."

That's Charlotte and John at the stage of first deterioration. The marriage, started with such hope and love by both, is coming apart at the seams, and John hasn't been an exploiter; far from it. If anyone has been exploited, he has. But it has worked two ways. Charlotte is trapped by what she felt was right; John is overwhelmed by responsibility.

Some Johns and Charlottes fight their way out of it. But most accept the situation. As the years go by Charlotte gets tighter and more harassed. Often her only way out of the situation is a constant aggressive attack on John. Much of the final resolution depends on John's success in the world. If he can sublimate his frustration and misery and plunge into work he may end up well-to-do. Well enough to find a mistress or a series of them and look to them for the love Charlotte denies him.

"I see Sarah a few times a week when I'm supposed to be entertaining out-of-town clients and she's all that keeps me sane. Sarah is everything Charlotte isn't. She's warm and loving and understanding. Even when we don't have sex and I just kick off my shoes and stretch out on her couch and talk to her, it's as if new life were pouring into me. It gets so I hate to go home and face Charlotte. I'm nothing to her, a meal ticket. I'm the kids' private-school-payer, her charge-account-settler. When she looks at me it's speculative. How much can I afford? Should we move to a new apartment? There's a co-op for sale. There's a sale at this store, a bargain at that one. Her eyes are like dollar signs, or numbers on a cash register."

Some day, when the kids are grown, or when he has had enough, the acute phase of the second-marriage syndrome will attack John, and he'll ask for a divorce and Charlotte will be bewildered, and then hurt, and then angry, often viciously angry. Enough to want to make John suffer in the one place she's used to hitting him, his wallet.

"She's an economic leech," John will say firmly, after the divorce settlement. "She always has been. She sucks the dollars out of me. Her support, the kids' support, extra for this, extra for that. She can't live now on twice what I made when we first had the kids. Sure, prices are up, but not by that much. She's out to get me. She couldn't get me in all the years of our marriage, and so she's determined to do it now."

Then with a sigh, "Thank God for Sarah."

But there were warnings. John could have seen ahead when he was still an adolescent, before he ever met Charlotte. John was dating then.

"It's damned unfair," he used to complain. "I haven't any more money than Ellen. If anything, she's better off. Her father gives her an allowance. But we go out to a movie and who pays the tab? I do. We eat dinner and I pay. If we go Dutch it's such a big thing I never hear the end of it. Not only from Ellen but from my own folks and my friends.

"I come into the house after a Dutch date, and my mother greets me with, 'Hello, the gigolo's home.' It's just not fair."

It's the Boy Who Pays

But John grew up in a different time. Is it still true today that the boy is stuck with the expenses of a date? A recent "rap" session with a group of boys at a small Ivy League college indicated that this is still the way things are.

"Sure, we're stuck with the expenses. We're used by the girls as someone to take them out. Our parents expect it and encourage it. I can always get money from them to date a girl. That's accepted. It's twice as hard to get half as much money when I want to get to a movie and dinner with another guy."

"We're expected to be creative thinkers. Ask a girl what she wants to do, and she'll pull this 'anything you want to do' shit. The onus is put on us to come up with an idea for the evening. If it doesn't work out, believe me they let us know later what they'd rather have done. Why can't a girl ever say, 'I want to do this. I want to go there.' In the end they'll get their way or make us suffer."

"They exploit us sexually. They play a neat game of come-on, being flirtatious and warm and yielding, and we're sucked in, and at the last minute when it looks like we've got it made, they draw back. 'Who me? Oh, no. Not that.'"

"They expect us to be masters at the whole game of sex. We don't know any more than they do, and we're just as scared. Oh, maybe a few of us are into this new sex-freedom business but believe me, most of us are as frightened of the whole thing as the girls are. Why do we have to be the experts? Why can't we be unsure and worried and still be accepted as men?"

"They use us to take them places. I as a boy don't mean anything. It's the wheels I can get hold of, the places I can take her to, the big shots I might know. I feel I'm some kind of a key she uses to get into places. What kind of a relationship is that?"

And looking back to a more tender age, how many boys of three or four or five have been removed from a quarrel and told, "No, you must not hit little girls. Even if they hit you first, you mustn't hit them. And if they do hit you and it hurts, you mustn't cry because boys don't cry."

Negative Differentiation

Purpose: To help the man and woman confront the negative effect our culture has had on their sexual differentiation.

The man takes a male doll and calls it MAN. The woman takes a female doll and calls it WOMAN. A competition is staged between MAN and WOMAN in which each describes the other sex in negative terms. For example:

> **He: Women are lousy drivers.**
> **She: Men are slobs.**
> **He: Women can't handle money.**
> **She: Men can't cope.**
> **He: Women gossip.**
> **She: Men are obscene.**

Suppose by some fantastic set of circumstances both husband and wife make it through the years of marriage without a divorce. Suppose John buries his resentment and finds, in his job, some of the satisfaction he never found at home. Suppose he even manages to build up a non-sexual relationship or a sexual one with his secretary, a relationship that gives him all the things he misses in Charlotte. And suppose Charlotte finds fulfillment at the League of Women Voters or the local church and in one way or another they manage to stay together until the kids grow up and leave. And John is finally given the symbolic gold watch by his outfit and retired. What happens then? John and Charlotte come face to face with each other and must once and for all learn to live together.

"I just can't get used to a man around the house every

day, under foot all the time! I just wish he had some place to go, something to do."

"I forgot what Charlotte was like. I used to think she was fun to talk to, full of bright ideas. I really looked forward to our getting to know each other again. My God, there's nothing to know. Her whole world is centered around the house, the kids, the grandchildren and the garden."

The Wasted Years

And John comes face to face with the terrible realization that all these years have been wasted, meaningless. "What did I live for? What did I kill myself for? To buy a life for Charlotte and the kids? What am I, a meal ticket and no more? Now I've finished working. I've retired and I've got nothing. A big nothing! I might just as well have done what these hippie kids do, throw off my shoes and go do my own thing. If I had done it back when I was twenty, I would have had some sort of a life to look back on. As it is, I've wasted time all my life, and now when I've finally got a handful of time I don't know what to do with it."

But John couldn't have dropped out back when he was twenty. Dropping out hadn't really been invented then. And even a dropout has to live within the framework of the society. Eventually most give in or sell out, usually by the time they're thirty. John was driven by his biological needs, and had few other options than marriage to some Charlotte.

For all the talk about women being exploited by men in our society, the raw fact is that man is fully exploited. For every case of a dominated woman, we can come up with a case of a dominated man. The voracious female forced into a domineering pattern is neither myth nor fiction. There is a Portnoy's mother, as we have seen in an earlier chapter; whether he's Jewish, Irish, or any other ethnic group. Heaven preserve all men from the WASP-dominating mother, she does it all with a smile instead of a knife.

We can find all sorts of excuses for women dominating men, but then there are equal excuses, including the biological one, for men dominating women.

In spite of the battle for domination we do get married because the sexual heat of an early marriage clouds the incompatibility. Do we wear "Barbie" and "Ken" masks to hide our real faces until the stress and strain of living together melts the masks?

Perhaps men and women were never meant to live together. There are penguins who come together at mating time and live in what appears to be the closest harmony and love, but only during the time they mate and raise fledgelings. As soon as the fledgelings are able to leave the colony the parent birds separate. And even during migrations they ignore each other. Behavioral scientists wonder, indeed, if these mated penguins could recognize each other when they are not in a mating state. Yet the next season the same penguins will get together to mate and to nest.

We can only compare the behavior of humans to the behavior of birds on two levels; if we want to search for the origin of certain traits, or if we wish to use symbolic analogies. Would it be logical for men and women to live together during the time they are mating and raising their children, then to separate? However, we do not, like birds, conceive each season, nor do our fledgelings leave the nest after one brief summer. They take off after twenty hard winters and by then we're in no condition to separate and mate again.

Except that in many cases this is just what does happen. The second-marriage syndrome is a perfect example of it. We stay together until our children are grown and independent, and then we separate like the birds. However, without actually following this mating-for-one-season pattern, we can take a useful, symbolic hint from these penguin colonies.

A recent article on happy marriages that have survived over the years noted a common factor in each. This was the ability of each of the partners to have independent interests. Husband and wife lived lives of their own, both sometimes had careers of their own. They went their separate ways except, like the penguins, when the time of mating was at hand.

8

Aggression and Submission

Luke and Rachel and Simon and Joan

Luke and Simon were close friends. They had known each other all through high school and had gone to the same state college. They were regular tennis partners on Saturday morning and they attended the same gym each Thursday after work. When Luke married Rachel, Simon was the best man, and a month later, when Simon married Joan, Luke stood in as his best man.

It wasn't surprising that when, for the summer months, Luke's uncle loaned him and Rachel a cabin fronting on a small natural lake, high in the Sierra Nevada Mountains, Luke enthusiastically invited Simon and Joan to share it.

"Man, it's like out-of-sight. Nothing but mountains and trees and clean water. You know, you can drink that lake water and it's purer than the stuff that comes out of the taps in the city. You guys have to come up there with us and share it. It's too much to use alone."

Rachel was equally enthusiastic. "Joan, you're my best

friend, and I have to be stuck away from everything in the back of God-knows-where, without even electricity, and only a pump in a miserable one-room cabin with a Coleman lantern and a stove, you've got to come with me or I'll go clean out of my tree!"

Simon and Joan agreed and the four took off in Luke's Volkswagen, the men in front and the girls in back, with all the equipment necessary to spend an isolated month on an ecology kick. Simon brought a Monopoly game, a huge sack of Granola for breakfast, and brown rice as a nourishing base for their meals. Fortunately there was a country store three miles down the mountain.

The month in the mountain worked into a pleasant daily routine, to Rachel's surprise. Every day one or the other couple would take a canoe out on the lake to give their friends a few hours of privacy, and Rachel and Joan began to fall slowly in love with nature.

But the evenings were a different problem. The one room contained only four cots, a table and chairs. They soon drifted into a standard routine, after the first week had thoroughly exhausted all their inventiveness. They sat around the table playing Monopoly by the light of the Coleman lantern.

By the end of the second week, a pattern began to emerge. It can only be described by what Simon called *Cutthroat Imperialist Monopoly.* "Monopoly can be a fun game, but not the way we began to play it," he said. "It became aggressive, ugly, almost vicious. Each of us was out to get the other. We would show each other no mercy. We would be cruel and vicious, all within the framework of the Monopoly game. We began to use expressions like 'I'll get that bastard tonight if it's the last thing I do.' 'I'll fix her with this, by God I will.' 'You want Boardwalk and Park Place—I'll see you bankrupt first.' 'You're on one of my hotels—pay through the nose, buddy!'"

"It used to frighten me," Rachel confided, "I never knew a game could be so sinister. There we were, the four of us, all sitting around the table, our eyes narrowed, our teeth gritted, ready to explode at one another at the drop of a hat, muttering under our breaths as if the game were the most important, the most serious thing in the world."

"Simon is normally the sweetest man I know," Joan said. "But during those games he was transformed. He used to scare me. I was actually afraid of him. He wouldn't give anyone a break—and talk about cornering every monopoly. . . ."

At the end of the month, the four of them drove down the mountain, Luke and Rachel in the front, Simon and Joan in the back, holding hands but silent. "You could have cut that silence with a knife," Rachel said.

"It's a funny thing," Simon told me later, describing that month, "we didn't speak to Luke and Rachel for almost a year afterwards. We were just so furious with them, though I'll never know why. I guess you just can't share a cabin with friends, not in such close quarters."

"But what about you and Joan?" I asked.

"Now that's a funny thing. Joan and I had had a lot of trouble with our marriage before that. On the outside it looked beautiful, and everybody thought we were such a great couple. But we were having it rough. I'm not sure we would have made it, yet that summer was like a tonic to us. We came down from that mountain a real married couple, and our marriage has been pretty good since. It was somehow as if we faced a lot of problems together and solved them, but we really didn't. I don't know why it happened that way, what with all the ugliness up in that cabin."

All the ugliness that Simon talked about was probably just what brought him and Joan closer together.

Learning from Fish

Konrad Lorenz, in one of the most significant books of this century, *On Aggression,* discussing the aggressive behavior of a small tropical fish, says ". . . analogous processes play a decisive role in the family and the social life of a great many higher animals and man." He goes on to say, "The problem of how to prevent intermarital fighting is solved in a truly remarkable way not only by not inhibiting the aggression elicited in each partner by the presence of the other, but by putting it to use in fighting the hostile neighbor."

All the ugliness of Simon and Joan's summer was directed toward the symbolic fight with the hostile neighbors, Rachel and Luke. Symbolic, because it was all in the framework of a fun game. And after all it was only a game. You can't really hurt someone with Monopoly. They spent their days pleasantly enough and there was rarely a harsh word between them, except during the nightly game. All their aggression came out then, directed toward the hostile neighbor.

Get the Guest

Purpose: To help the man and woman achieve solidarity by confronting a common enemy.

The man takes one male doll and calls it HOST. He then takes a second male doll, calling it GUEST. The woman takes a female doll and calls it HOSTESS. She then takes a second female doll and calls it MRS. GUEST.

HOST and HOSTESS pretend GUESTS are their best friends, isolated with them in a cabin by a snow storm.

HOST and HOSTESS try to establish a bond between themselves by attacking the two GUESTS.

But returning to Lorenz, I had the good fortune to observe recently the same behavior that led him to his conclusions about the tropical fish. I was on vacation at a West Indies island and I discovered the wonders of snorkeling. With flippers and snorkel mask, I spent hours hovering over the reefs off the western coast of the island. I watched, with all the greediness of a seasoned voyeur, the teeming life of the reef.

The uninitiated can have no idea of the fantastic variety of fish, or the brilliant color of those dwelling in the coral. For the first few days of snorkeling I could only give in to a drunken kind of reef-watching where every turn and bend and cranny in the coral revealed some new and different life.

But after a while the endless variety becomes natural, and you begin to notice the activities of the individual

| 127

brilliantly colored tropical fish. One blue fish in particular seemed to be a feisty little fellow, always darting out at any fish that invaded his particular little cranny.

Good, I thought. I'm learning a lesson of nature. This fish defends his home against all strangers. Then with something of a start I became aware that he was not defending his home against strangers at all. He ignored the strangers. The black and yellow tiger fish swam by serenely, and he paid them no mind. A blue and black striped fellow got right to the heart of his territory and he ignored him.

But let another blue fish exactly like himself come near, and zap, he's darting at him, driving him off. And I was suddenly aware that these ugly, aggressive little fellows only attack their own species.

My vacation was not long enough, nor was I an experienced enough observer, to discover the other facts that Lorenz makes about these brilliantly colored coral fish. They are, he notes, only brilliantly colored before they mate, and after that their color fades. It is a flag to incite an aggressive action in others. Each blue fish reacts angrily to any other blue fish like himself. Any child who has raised Siamese fighting fish knows that if you put one in a tank with a mirror he will try to fight his own reflection.

Why this aggressive behavior? Why should one fish chase away any fish of his own species that invades his territory? Obviously it is a device of nature to scatter the fish over a large area instead of letting them cluster in one spot and eat it bare. But when the fish gets ready to reproduce, this angry behavior could become harmful. He might attack and destroy his would-be mate. So with maturity the fish lose their color, and also lose their aggressive impulse against the color, accepting each other. After spawning, however, they change back to their brilliant hues and scatter.

The aggression that separates the fish once they have mated is a necessity of life. It forces them out over larger territories. As Lorenz notes, aggression is "an essential part of a life-preserving organization of instincts." Even if it functions in the wrong way sometimes, it is still a valuable instinct. Any instinct or drive can go rotten.

Fear, Aggression and Sexuality

We all live with aggression, and we all channel it outward in different ways for safety's sake. If, while driving, we are cut off rudely by another driver, we will almost always respond with a show of anger and fury out of all proportion to the stimulation. The show of anger is safe because we are in our car and cannot reach the other driver nor can he reach us. At best we can exchange a few soul-satisfying insults and drive away. Only rarely do actual fights erupt from such situations, and when they do they are often deadly. The participants just do not know or cannot learn the rules. Their own aggression is too close to the surface, too uncontrollable.

Lorenz, considering the drive toward aggression in animals, has come up with a fascinating concept that eventually applies to humans as well. In the cichlid, a spiny-finned, fresh water fish he sees three great drives: fear, aggression and sexuality. The male and female of these fish are exactly alike in appearance, and many behavioral scientists have wondered how the boy-fish know the girl-fish, and vice versa. That knowledge, Lorenz suggests, is based on these three drives. The male fish cannot feel sexuality and fear at the same time. He must feel one or the other. The slightest touch of fear extinguishes his sexuality. The female has the same relationship between aggression and sexuality. She cannot be sexual and aggressive. If she has any aggression to her partner, she is just not sexual. A note here for human wives!

On the other side of the coin, the male can be aggressive and sexual and be happy with it. The female can be fearful and sexual at the same time.

What do we have here? A four-cornered formula for compatibility. Alas, these are only fish. Perhaps, though, there is some relationship in this situation to human behavior. We'll consider this later on.

Lorenz, as many behavioral scientists do, warns us against confusing animal behavior with human morality. The animal behaves the way he does because of built-in instincts. A line of birds, for example, sitting on a telephone wire will space themselves out just as a line of people waiting to cross the street will space themselves out. The spacing among birds turns out to be just that distance away from each other that will prevent each from being pecked by his neighbor. Birds have an instinct to peck any other bird, even of their own kind, that gets near them. It is a remnant of the same instinct that causes the coral fish to attack his fellow.

In humans the desire for privacy, the need for spatial zones around the body, exists for a completely different reason. Edward T. Hall, in *The Hidden Dimension,* sees the reason as an outgrowth of man's territorial requirement.

A human does not behave the way he does because of instinct. He bases his actions on reason, yet his reasoning is only the visible tip of the behavioral iceberg. Below the reason is the vast shadowy bulk of man's drives. These drives impel him into action, and he changes or adapts that action within the framework of his ability to overcome the drives.

Redirection: Turning Our Emotions

Man has inherited his drives, just as he inherits the color of his hair, the length of his legs or the shape of his nose. This is a biological inheritance, and rules have been laid down for such inheritance. However man, unlike most animals, also has a cultural inheritance. These laws are different than the laws of his biological inheritance, but no less certain. The man born into a society that has invented the wheel, pottery, the printing press and the lever will inherit these goodies, just as the man who is born into the society that has invented the atomic bomb will also inherit that.

It is also true that the man born into our society of fixed values will inherit these values. In our society, the role that each sex must play is just as surely inherited as hair color, eye shape and a tendency toward Mongolism. On the positive side, we can change our biological inheritance. Biologists are learning how to examine the fluid in which the baby floats and determine if its genetic makeup is desirable.

| 131

If it isn't they may abort it. Some day we may be able to eliminate Mongolism with this method.

Behavioral scientists are also examining the relationships between the sexes with a view to changing them, and it is highly likely that someday they will change them. But here and now we can only use a limited number of techniques for changing basic drives.

One of these techniques is redirection. For example, a friend of ours coughs or sneezes during a show and we feel an unreasoning fury toward him. One of our children picks his nose, or another splits the ends of her hair, and we feel irritated out of all proportion to the act. But we deflect our irritation and turn it into something more honorable and less petty. We use redirection. We search for some method of criticism that implies honorable concern with the individual. "Stop picking your nose or you'll infect yourself." "Your hair will stop growing if you keep splitting the ends." "That's a terrible cough. Maybe you'd better go home at the first intermission." I yell at the idiot driving that auto because he's a menace on the highway, not because he has cut me off personally.

This trick of "turning" or redirecting an emotion, is one of the basic concepts of interpersonal relationships. We can discharge our fury at another person by slamming a table instead. In fact, one type of encounter session suggests hitting a pillow furiously while we scream out all the anger we would ordinarily feel for our mother, father, sister, brother, wife, husband, or even children.

This harmless discharge of the emotions is part of the popular new primal scream therapy and all of it is based on some variation of turning or redirecting our basic emotions. The true story, about the two couples in a mountain cabin, with which I opened this chapter was a perfect example of the discharge of normal aggression built up within a marriage. Simon and Joan wondered why their marriage went so well after that summer, but an educated guess would be that together they found a mutual aggression against their friends.

The old song about marriage could be easily and truly paraphrased as "Love and aggression go together like an encounter session."

Love Among the Geese

Lorenz said that poet and psychoanalyst alike have long known how close love and hate are. We know that also the object of our love is nearly always, in an ambivalent way, an object of our aggression too. This brings to mind an attempt of Norman Mailer in his book *An American Dream* to equate aggression and love, a theme that has obviously facinated and intrigued him. His own life includes an episode in which he knifed his wife.

But this is hardly a new theme in literature or poetry. Writers have always recognized the ambivalence of love and hate. Oscar Wilde wrote, *Yet each man kills the thing he loves,/By each let this be heard,/. . . The coward does it with a kiss,/The brave man with a sword.*

Lorenz, who has done so much work with the Greylag goose, explains just how close aggression is to love in these animals, how, in fact, aggression is really only another face of love. He tells in great detail of the *triumph ceremony*

| 133

with which geese in love communicate that love to each other.

The triumph ceremony is based on a redirection of aggression, and many of the gestures the geese use were originally threatening gestures, now modified so that they have become appeasing instead. One goose cannot hurt another when faced with an appeasing gesture. In one incident described by Lorenz, two geese who have lived together for many years become completely caught up in a triumph ceremony, proclaiming their love to each other. The ceremony gets wilder and wilder as they get carried away, and then, in error, one goose uses a threatening gesture instead of an appeasing one and inadvertently releases the other goose's aggression.

The result? He is caught by the neck in a real attack, and in turn catches his mate. The symbolic triumph ceremony ends and a furious and real battle ensues, almost a battle to the death.

Most animals, like the geese, use appeasing gestures as a sort of body language. Our cranky old Puli bitch, eight years old, was faced recently with a visiting puppy who wanted to play. The Puli gave the puppy a few disdainful sniffs, then turned away. The puppy leaped up and nipped her rear.

Our Puli, furious, turned with a snarl and bared her fangs, and the puppy promptly rolled on its back in a groveling gesture of appeasement. The Puli's aggression was blocked. Unable to hurt the puppy, she turned away; at this point the puppy promptly jumped up and nipped her again. It went on like that until we finally took pity on the Puli and separated them. The point is that the Puli's aggression could not exist in the face of the puppy's appeasement. This is one of the basic laws of nature. Aggression in animals, aggression toward one's own species, is usually turned aside by appeasement. When the angry coral fish dashes at its mate in an aggressive fury, the mate makes an appeasing gesture and the angry fish turns aside. The elaborate courting dances of birds are nothing but appeasement ceremonies to familiarize them with each other before mating.

And in humans, do we have the equivalent of appeasement ceremonies?

In a typical man-woman encounter, the man "comes on strong," aggressive and domineering. What does the woman do? She appeases, or in more familiar terms, she flirts. She becomes coy, half lowers her eyelids, turns her head to one side (like the goose exposing her vulnerable throat) and goes through all the body-language gestures of appeasement. These actions are so typical that they hardly bear description. Everyone is familiar with them.

Women's liberation maintains that feminine coyness and flirting or masculine aggressiveness are culturally learned. According to them, "We all learn our roles and play them because the society demands it of us."

There may be a good deal of truth in this view, but it is also true that many girl-babies start the flirting and coyness at so early an age that there is considerable doubt about it being learned. We all know fathers of baby girls who say, "There's no doubt about that little one. She was flirting before she could stand!" And they mean it. Boy-babies, too, show their true colors at an early age. Studies have found them more hyperactive, harder to handle, more aggressive than little girls.

There is no doubt that some part of personality is inborn, just as there is no doubt that another part is environmentally produced. But how much femininity and how much masculinity is born into a human being and how much is picked up from the environment still remain to be decided. What we do know is that it isn't all of one or all of the other. We are a mixture of our culture plus ourselves.

The Janitor's Boy Syndrome

Lorenz guesses that love arose, in many cases, from aggression within a species. He also suggests that while aggression can exist without love, "there is no love without aggression." It is this conclusion that has made many people reject his work. It is tremendously difficult to accept such a tie-in of love and aggression. But we know that man is aggressive. We know that in primitive, proto-human days he needed both strength and aggression to survive. The man with the greatest strength and the strongest aggressive drives made out better than his fellows.

This edge of survival was enough to allow evolution to select aggression and strength as two extremely desirable traits. It was certainly enough to hook these two traits onto sexual selection. The women who picked the strongest, most aggressive men had the best chance of surviving.

The two traits would inevitably be built into human men since those who were weak and unaggressive would not be likely to find mates. In the same way, a need for aggression and strength would automatically be built into the woman who did the selecting. In her eyes masculinity would inevitably be tied up with aggression and strength, and sexuality would come alive under their impact.

The old cartoon of the caveman dragging his mate off by her hair has elements of truth. Only elements, however, for his aggression would have to be directed past his woman to the world at large. But the caveman approach has lived on in women's fantasy. Every teen-age girl dreams of being carried off by a bold lover who will sweep aside the objections of her family, her friends and herself. In her dream she whispers, "No, no!" while she clings to him frantically.

How else explain the appeal of all those heroes of stage and screen who have a touch of latent cruelty in their makeup Rudolph Valentino, James Mason, Richard Burton, Yul Brynner—they were all a little frightening to the heroine, but the women wanted to shiver in delightful anticipation as their sullen-eyed hero strolled through the moors, the western streets or downtown London.

How else explain the popularity among women of the gothic novels of today, all rewrites of the basic Brontë tale—the innocent young girl, the grim, frightening older man, the wild suspense while the reader is kept on the edge of her chaise wondering if the hero (?) is really the hero or, as he so obviously seems, the villain.

The best heroes, we know, have a touch of coldness in them, a touch of cruelty, a healthy sprinkling of aggression and they are lightly flavored with sullenness and served up in a taciturn physical dish of dark, moody eyes and a brooding brow.

It's the Janitor's Boy Syndrome. Remember Natalie Crane's poem about the janitor's boy? ". . . He'll carry me off, I know he will,/For his hair is exceedingly red,/And the only thing that occurs to me/Is to dutifully shiver in bed."

And when the stereotype goes a bit wrong, it ends up in male sadism and the woman reacts with gleeful masochism, and still another syndrome is born.

No fictional stereotype could exist through so many books and plays and poems and novels unless there were tremendous elements of truth in it. Strength and aggression are what the woman wants. We better believe it. Women's Lib will never change that. Indeed all Women's Lib will do is strengthen the stereotype. The liberation woman will end up fantasizing men strong and aggressive enough to subdue *her*, and that will take a lot of man!

Reason Versus Aggression

But if all of this is so, why aren't all real men equal to the fantasy men of fiction? What has happened to natural selection? Where are the results of millions of years of survival of the fittest? Why aren't all men strong and aggressive? We know for sure that they aren't—there are many weak men and many unaggressive men. Why have they survived?

They have managed to survive and perhaps outnumber the aggressive ones because another factor entered into the whole selection process when man developed a brain. That factor was reason. The prize no longer went to the strongest or to the most aggressive. It went instead to the cleverest, to the one who could reason best.

It was this reasoning ability that eventually taught predatory man how to enslave his partner—and inevitably it will teach him how to free her. We are human, but not yet humane. We are in the process of evolving, and the result of our evolution will surely be far better than we are, a wiser more humane human.

But in the meanwhile we are men and women, and reason is as important a survival factor to us as either aggression or strength. In fact it may be a far more important factor. The reasoning man can usually outwit the strong, aggressive one, as witness David and Goliath. So, on a survival level, intelligence counts as strongly as aggression—perhaps more. I certainly hope so for the future of mankind.

But on a deeper level, on a sexual level, evolution has linked aggression to sex with very strong bonds. There are two aspects to this linkage. In one case aggression can strengthen the tie between a married couple when it is directed outward at the world. In this case the aggressive drive is often changed and distorted to the two-against-the-world syndrome. "You and I, love, are all that count. The hell with everybody else."

There are good and bad aspects of this syndrome. It can, as we saw in the case of Joan and Simon, strengthen and improve a marriage. But the danger is that it can also isolate a marriage and create a mistrustful, suspicious couple. At its best, I believe it can be a source of strength to each member of the marriage. When something goes wrong, properly directed aggression can unite a couple and water away whatever tension there may be between them.

The other function of aggression lies in the act of sex. Earlier in the chapter we considered the cichlid fish and its fascinating linkage of sex, aggression and fear. The significant part of this linkage is that the male can be aggressive and sexual, but aggressiveness in the female turns off sexuality. The opposite is true of the male; fear turns off sexuality.

Command Performance

Purpose: To force the woman to explore what would happen to her own feelings were she allowed to become the aggressor in a sexual partnership.

Round one: The man takes one male and one female doll. He calls the male doll ME and the female doll SHE. The man acts both roles. SHE orders ME to perform sexually. Only ME expresses his feelings as the performance progresses.

Round two: The woman takes the female doll and labels it ME, then labels the male doll HE. ME orders HE to perform, and only ME expresses her feelings as the performance continues.

The Land That Time Forgot

Let me elaborate on this with the example of a land that time forgot, marsupial Australia. Every native inhabitant of Australia, except man and dog, is marsupial, a primitive form of mammalian life. We are all familiar with the marsupial kangaroo and our own American marsupial, the opossum. These animals have no placenta. The baby crawls out of the mother's womb while still undeveloped and finishes its fetal development in the mother's marsupium or pouch. Here it nurses its way to maturity.

Placental mammals are ahead of marsupials in the evolutionary game, and the baby develops completely before it is born. This extra survival value of placental mammals has allowed them to replace marsupial mammals all over the world, except for a few hold-outs like our opossum and the entire isolated continent of Australia.

The point I want to make is that, in Australia, marsupial life mimicked placental life in the rest of the world. As a result Australia has a marsupial cat, a marsupial wolf, a marsupial mole, mouse, groundhog and even a duplicate of the flying squirrel. They are all physically similar to the placental cats, wolves, moles, mice, groundhogs and squirrels we know.

However, and this is a big however, they are all examples of convergent evolution. They are not closely related at all. In fact the marsupial cat is incredibly farther away, in evolution, from our placental cat, than our cat is from a mouse or a man.

What has happened is that similar environments have molded similar life forms from completely different stock. Environment is the great sculptor, the magnificent creative force in evolution. And it works not only on the physical appearance of life, but on the psychological drives as well. The instincts and drives of life are molded by the environment, even as the shape of life is molded.

Cultural Charades

The shuffling of the three traits, sexuality, aggression and fear, in the fish is matched by a convergent evolutionary shuffling of these traits in the human. A girl and a boy making love on the living-room couch is a classic example. There is a creaking on the stairs, and the boy leaps back.

"What is it?" he whispers.

Annoyed, the girl says, "It's nothing. My father is upstairs."

"What if he comes down?"

"Oh, for heaven's sake, come on!"

"I can't. I just can't do anything when I'm scared. Why the hell can't we ever make love when we won't be interrupted?"

Or take the wife of the henpecked husband who tells her friend, "Sex with Harry is something I put up with because he needs it. I don't feel a thing." The aggressive, dominating wife seldom does feel sexual stimulation because sex and aggression don't go well together in a woman. Instead she fakes it, "For Harry's sake."

Or take the tritest, oldest situation between men and women, the charade between the girl who "doesn't want to" and the boy who does. In the end sex is accomplished with the boy forcing himself on the girl and the girl protesting weakly, but guiding him in at the moment of penetration. The charade, in which both are accomplices, is played out to certain rigid rules. The girl must protest, but not strongly enough to discourage him. The boy must persist. The girl combines a symbolic fear with sexuality, the boy a symbolic aggression with sexuality.

In no way do I mean to imply that this charade is rape. Rape is a part of the aggression-fear-sexuality triad, but a perverted travesty of it, just as sado-masochism is another perversion. The girl who fantasizes about rape is like the homosexual man who fantasizes about being pierced through the body with a spear. Neither would allow the act to happen if they could stop it. These are only symbolic fantasies. The boy who "forces" sex with the girl is different. He is playing a cultural charade.

The lesson that we, as humans, can learn from the aggression-fear-sexuality triad in fish is that evolution has, in many disparate species from fish to man, selected sexual aggression as the man's role in sex and sexual submissiveness as the woman's role.

Now this does not, in any way, negate an active sex role on the part of the woman, or a passive role on the part of the man. Activity does not preclude submissiveness, nor does passivity preclude aggression. They can exist together, if not at the same time, then at different times during the same sexual act. In oral sex the man who is made love to by the woman does not "submit" to that lovemaking, any more than the woman making love uses aggression to subdue the man.

The most misunderstood term of all in sexuality is submission. It has reached the point where it is almost a dirty word in our culture, and yet it needn't be. Sexual submission like sexual aggression is simply a function of human sexuality, as it is of most, if not all, vertebrate sexuality.

We can understand its interplay in animals. The female plays a submissive role, the male an aggressive one, and they must act this way if sex is to be culminated. It is most obvious between a mare and a stallion, a bull and a heifer or a bitch and a dog. But even in cats, where mating involves furious fighting on the part of the female, the final act is one of submission, perhaps more obviously so because of the fighting.

The male and female sexual organs in the higher animals

are built to accommodate these aggressive-submissive roles. A woman cannot aggressively make love to a man unless she in some way arouses him to aggression, nor can a man be submissive in sexual union. The very acts of erection and penetration are aggressive acts; the act of being penetrated is a submissive one.

One of the basic tenets of Masters and Johnson's work in curing sexual problems has been an attempt to convince the man that he is not being ordered to perform. Such aggressive manipulation on the part of the woman guarantees that he will lose his erection and become impotent. Yet the woman can be taught to make love actively and achieve the erection in her mate.

The aggressive-submissive part of sex is a biological fact, and there is no realistic reason why we should deny it, except that in some way sexual submission to many women has come to be tied up with sexual exploitation. This is indeed a different matter and one that has been covered in some depth earlier in this book. Sexual exploitation is at the root of the incompatibility between the sexes, whether it be exploitation by the man or by the woman.

Sexual submission and sexual aggression, handled properly, are the keys to overcoming incompatibility.

9

Aggression and Sex

The Young Violents

Recently a group of researchers, Drs. Robert M. Rose, Irwin S. Berstein and Leo Kreuz, made some curious discoveries about the hormonal differences in men and women. There is a direct relationship, they discovered, between male sex hormones and aggressiveness. In an experimental monkey colony, they found that the most aggressive male monkeys secreted the largest amounts of the male sex hormone, testosterone. For these monkeys, the biological fact of masculinity was tied to aggressiveness. Is this also true for man?

The researchers conducted a prison study at the Maryland Institute for Defective Delinquents, where aggression often takes a pathological turn. They found a very definite connection between aggression and testosterone. "Young Violents," prisoners arrested before they were eighteen years old for crimes of aggression, assault and attempted murder, secreted more testosterone than the other prisoners.

Additional experiments with army groups proved that, under stress or fear, men secrete less testosterone, indicating that stress and aggression do not go together. With the lowering of testosterone, the three researchers said, "Interviews with the men also showed that sex was the furthest thing from their minds."

What we have here is the beginning of a scientific basis for the theoretical relationship between aggression, fear and sexuality in men. The study indicates that testosterone, the male hormone, is linked to aggression; the more testosterone a man has, the more aggressive he is. The study also shows that under stress, sexual desire is lowered. Lessened aggression also seems to indicate lessened sexual desire. If further studies confirm these preliminary findings, we will be well on our way to confirming the link between aggression and sex in men.

The Reproduction Drive

There may be similar studies in progress on the role of female hormones and sexual submissiveness. As yet I have heard of no reported results in this area, but there have been many studies done to indicate that the female hormone estrogen is very closely tied up with sexual desire. It certainly influences the female sex organs. For example, the lining of a woman's vagina is directly affected by her production of estrogen. We know this because of what happens to the lining after the menopause. It is a peculiarity of evolution that once a woman stops having children, she is considered obsolete by nature. Nature (to use this anthropomorphic concept for whatever force moves life along the evolutionary track) is concerned primarily with reproduction. Every element of life is geared to promoting reproduction.

Those of us who tend toward religion like to see a touch of the divine in our sexual ecstasy, but the down-to-earth biologist sees such ecstasy as a sly device to force life into reproduction. Nature is obsessed with the need to reproduce, to scatter life. She fills us with drives, the maternal drive, the aggressive drive, the sexual drive, all to further the spread of life. A man produces millions of sperm so that one may reach the egg. A fish produces thousands of eggs so that a few may live. Nature is enormously profligate, and once she has reached her goal, she ruthlessly and cruelly loses interest in the organism.

The lady spider of some species will eat her mate as he begins to copulate with her and she will eagerly finish her meal while he, just as eagerly, driven by ruthless nature, finishes his copulation. His lower body will continue the job while his upper half goes down his wife's gullet. Nature has lost interest in the male spider once he has started his job of reproduction, though she has built in rigid guarantees that once started he will finish.

In the same way, nature ensures that the male of the human species continues to receive his supply of testosterone long past his youth. He must be equipped to feed and protect his family, and testosterone is part of the equipment. It gives him muscular strength and an aggressive drive. One of the physical evidences of a high supply of testosterone, incidentally, is baldness. There seems a connection between certain types of baldness and high male hormone levels.

Researchers believe there is also a connection between genital size and testosterone, but this is less clear. Some far-out theorists have even speculated that the sexual attractiveness of bald-headed men is based on their supposedly enlarged genitals, but this is all in the neighborhood of myth and fantasy. What is certain is that testosterone levels remain high in many men long after estrogen levels have died away in women.

When women finish their child-bearing years, usually in their late forties, uncompromising nature shrugs and cuts off their supply of eggs. Since both estrogen and eggs come from functioning ovaries, nature also cuts off women's supply of estrogen. This induces that woeful time of life known as the menopause, a pause in menstruation, for menstruation is tied to the production of eggs. The woman's entire body has been kept youthful and sexually attractive by estrogen. It has fleshed out her tissues, strengthened her bones, lifted her breasts and smoothed her face. With its diminution, old age begins to set in. The breasts sag, the face wrinkles and even the bones grow brittle. Callous nature doesn't care. The woman's usefulness is over, and she is no longer important to the spread of life.

But what happens to her sexual organs with this loss of estrogen? The tissue of the vagina thins out so much that it may tear during intercourse. Here is a warning from nature that sexuality is about to end, and it accompanies—or perhaps causes—a general psychological despondence in menopause women. Many of them lose their interest in sex at this time in life.

Yet if the post-menopause woman takes estrogen pills, her vaginal lining thickens and recovers its natural state. Her sexual desire also returns. Often many of the other good feelings of her pre-menopausal years also come back. So there is a connection between female sexual hormones and sexual functioning in women, just as there is a connection between the male sexual hormone and sexual functioning in men.

What scientists are finding is a reliable biological foundation for the concept that in man there seems to be the same four-cornered relationship among the elements, sex, aggression, fear and submission as has been observed in the cichlid fish. But sexual aggression, which can provide an enriching human experience must not be confused with sexual domination.

Domination and Aggression

Sexual domination, unlike sexual aggression, does not contribute to mutual satisfaction. It often satisfies only the dominating member. As a case in point, take the story of Laura and Norman. They have been married for over ten years, and they have a nine-year-old girl.

Norman is a bright, intelligent young executive in a promising industry, and his future is assured. "If only things at home were as good."

But what's wrong at home? Laura is a lovely woman, still attractive in her late thirties, clever and fun to be with. Their little girl, Nina, is unspoiled and even at nine is a talented artist. What could be wrong with such a couple?

"Frankly," Norman admitted to a family counselor, "I don't know what's wrong. All I know is that something is eating Laura, and it's spoiling our marriage. That's the whole of it."

"If you want the plain truth," Laura said suddenly, "it's sex."

"But we have sex," Norman protests. "A darned good sex life. We've always had one."

"Your idea of sex," Laura snapped, "is doing your own thing—frequently. For all I feel or you care, I might be a lump of clay."

"Well . . ." Norman paused for a long moment. "Women just don't feel sex the way men do."

"That's not true. I have feelings. You're not the first man I've ever slept with, though you were the last. I used to enjoy sex with other men."

"That's a hell of a thing to say. Don't you enjoy it with me?"

"No! I enjoy your enjoyment, but I don't enjoy it." Laura began to cry. "But I love you! I always have. It's just—oh, what's the use of discussing it? I can't make you see my point of view."

But this time Norman wanted to see, and he listened to Laura and the family counselor. The problem between them, the counselor pointed out, was Norman's confusion about the differences between aggression and domination. Norman dominated Laura sexually and in other ways, but it was the sexual domination that she couldn't take any longer.

"Dominate her how?" Norman asked in bewilderment.

Norman, the counselor explained, had sex when he wanted it. His prime concern was with his own pleasure, the relief of his feelings, the satisfaction of his tension. His ideas about women in general strengthened this view. He saw Laura as someone to be used—"Women just don't feel sex the way men do." This conviction gave him the green light to do as he pleased because he believed Laura wouldn't enjoy sex in any case.

Norman, an intelligent man, was simply the product of a completely male-dominated and male-oriented upbringing. His parents had always accepted male domination as proper, and had brought Norman up with this attitude. Norman's intelligence, however, allowed him to understand the situation between himself and Laura once it had surfaced, and it also allowed him to work it out. But here the problem became involved.

"I think it would have been better," Laura told their therapist bitterly some months later, "if Norman and I had left well enough alone."

"What's happened," Norman said unhappily, "is that most of the time, now, I just can't do anything. I guess I'm impotent."

Fortunately their therapist was both understanding and experienced. He explained that the impotence was a temporary problem, and was based only on a fear of failure, started, in fact, by Norman's questioning his own sexual role. "At the heart of the problem," the therapist said, "there's still a confusion between aggression and domination. When you stopped dominating Laura, you also stopped being aggressive. You can be aggressive without dominating. That's what you have to learn."

Norman was able to learn it, and he and Laura worked out their problem. It was in the natural order of things that Laura's own participation in curing Norman involved her psychologically in their sexual action to the point where she was able to experience orgasm. Norman, finally understanding the difference between aggression and domination, was able to separate the two and discover the deeper joy of aggressive sexual relations without domination, with Laura sharing in the experience instead of being used solely for his satisfaction.

10

Sexual Equality: The Great Mistake

Hormones and Chromosomes

Let's take a further biological look at the two sexes, and if possible, rid ourselves of all emotion and distortion. We know that there are physical differences between the sexes, and most of these differences are too obvious to be listed. There are also differences in strength. No one can deny that the average man is stronger than the average woman. The United States Department of Labor has noted that the strength of the average woman is a little more than half that of the average man. There is no record of a woman's beating a man in any feat or game requiring physical skill and exertion.

This difference in strength is not only true for humans, but for almost all mammals. The males are often bigger and usually stronger than the females. Their muscles are bulkier because of the male hormone testosterone. This is why, before puberty, before the testosterone starts flowing, a boy's muscles are as long and graceful as a woman's. In transsexual operations, when men are castrated to become pseudo-women, they are given estrogen, the female hormone, to counteract the effects of testosterone and increase their breast size and smooth out their muscles.

The hormonal balance of women is more delicate than that of men, and it is more easily troubled. A woman's metabolism is different too, and because of this women are usually a few degrees cooler than men and may require less food.

The average man outclasses the average woman physically. But is he biologically stronger?

Not one bit. From the womb to the tomb he is weaker, less resistant to disease and more prone to defects. This is probably due to the fact that genetically boys are weaker than girls.

Why genetically? Well, boys have less chromosomal material than girls. Girls have a full pack of forty-eight chromosomes. Boys have forty-seven chromosomes plus a fragment of the forty-eighth. This fragment is called the Y chromosome.

Every trait in our body, from eye color to toe shape, is governed by our genes, tiny segments of chromosomal material. Each trait is acted on by a pair of matching genes on matching chromosomes. All the chromosomes act in pairs —all but the poor Y chromosome. It pairs up with a fully developed chromosome called the X chromosome. Women have two Xs, men have an X and a Y.

Since human traits are caused by the actions of pairs of

genes on matching chromosomes, and most genes are healthy, we have some insurance that each trait will be healthy or normal. Genes for healthy traits are stronger than genes for unhealthy or abnormal traits. If two matching genes are on matching chromosomes, and one is normal and one abnormal, the normal gene will often mask the abnormal one, dominate it, and the trait will be normal.

But on the XY pair of chromosomes in men a different situation exists. There aren't enough genes on the Y fragment to match all of those on the X, and therefore many X genes have no good partner to tone down their possibly bad action. Statistically, this makes for more abnormal genes in men than in women, and therefore a weaker biological makeup, despite man's gift of stronger bones and muscles.

More boy-babies die before birth than girl-babies, and male deaths exceed female deaths at birth and after. It has also been estimated by the United States Bureau of Vital Statistics that 25 percent more boy-babies are born prematurely. Among boys there is a higher incidence of congenital malformation, circulatory and respiratory diseases, digestive diseases, infections, parasites and viral diseases. Indeed there is hardly any disease or defect which doesn't cause more destruction in boy-babies than in girls. This is strong indication of a biological difference, a built-in weakness probably due to the genetic difference between men and women.

This is a bit hard to accept in view of the fact that men are consistently so much physically stronger than women, but let's consider another aspect of the differences between the sexes. Work at the Yale Clinic of Child Development indicates that even before the first year of life is over, boys are ahead of girls in locomotor development and in any movement involving muscular strength or physical activity. Girls, however, as we noted before, are ahead of boys in fine motor development which affects the ability to do clever things with their hands.

Less Brawn, More Brains?

Physical differences are all well and good, but what about mental differences between the sexes? What about the ability to think and to reason?

I was recently invited to address a meeting of Mensa, the high IQ society, and I was struck by the fact that the audience was heavily male. The total membership, I was told later, was also weighted with men.

"We have to face up to the fact that there are more men than women with high IQs," one of the members told me. "Studies have proved it."

But have they?

As intelligence tests were originally constructed (the Binet-Simon, and the Stanford and Otis revisions) boys did better on some questions and girls did better on others. To compensate, the tests were adjusted to give boys and girls an equal chance. To quote Professor Quinn McNeman of Stanford University, they have eliminated "the test items which yield larger sex differences, and by this method may be able to dispense with separate norms."

If boys and girls test differently, in what part of the test are girls better? They excel in test items involving esthetic response, matching colors, discrimination in pictures, choice of words, vocabulary and copying from memory. Boys excel in mechanical ability, structural skills, mathematical reasoning, understanding abstract words and deciphering absurd situations. (Is this why men think they have a better sense of humor?)

Does all this make that much difference? A long-range study of high IQ children found that as they grew older the girls began to fall behind in relative achievement. Professor Lewis M. Terman, who started the study, reported at one point, "Boys not only become increasingly more likely than girls to have a high IQ as they advance in age, but they are more likely than girls to retain the high IQ earlier evidenced." This may have some bearing on Mensa's larger male membership.

Why should girls be less likely to retain a higher IQ? Perhaps they are conditioned to be less bright than men. Certainly all the books that offer advice to girls suggest that they try to make men feel superior. This is what the man-woman relationship in our society is based on. Make a man secure by letting him be smarter, or let him think he's smarter. This may well be evidence of a confusion between submission and lack of intelligence and between aggression and intelligence. We may subtly recognize the need for aggressiveness in men and try substituting intelligence for it, while women may feign a lack of intelligence for submission.

Perhaps conditioning isn't the total answer. There are great glandular differences between men and women. These differences become obvious at puberty—and this is the time when girls begin to drop behind in IQ measurement. Could there be a hormonal basis for the IQ differences? Or are women just not as intelligent as men?

Amram Scheinfeld, in his fine study of the sexes, *Women and Men,* says:

No intelligence test exists, or ever will be devised, which can accurately measure the relative mental capacities of men and women. No intelligence test ever can be devised which will prove that the mental capacities of men and women are quantitatively equal or unequal.

He goes on to say that no test can be devised to prove that men are superior to women or women to men in intelligence. "Anyone who doubts this should try to prove that blue is superior as a color to red, or the shape of an apple is superior to the shape of a pear."

What is more important than speculation on which sex is stronger, or which sex is smarter, is a consideration of the fact that each sex is different. We all know this, but we have been trapped into forgetting it by the cry for equality between the sexes. Equality is, plainly, the wrong word, and the struggle for equality, therefore, a false battle. Red is not "equal" to blue, and a pear is not "equal" to an apple —unless we are talking about an equality of merit. Of course men and women are equal in that sense. But that is not where the argument is at.

The Soviet Experiment

The experience of the Soviet Union gives us hints of this. After the revolution there was an attempt there to legislate equality between the sexes. The Soviet constitution said, "Women in the USSR are accorded equal rights with men in all spheres of economic, state, cultural, social and political life."

The "equal rights" were evident from the very beginning in their attempt to wipe out all restrictions on the division of labor between the sexes. Before World War II things began to look good for women. Women in the Soviet Union made up more than half of all the doctors, a third of all workers in the metal, oil and chemical industries, a quarter of the iron, steel and coal workers and one fifth of the engineers. In addition they worked on collective farms, railroads and even on ships.

Yet in the beginning there was an awareness of the special nature of women, an awareness of the "inequality" of the sexes. An attempt was made to protect women from heavy work that might keep them from having healthy children.

In the war years women served in the army, but almost exclusively behind the front, as our own WACs did. They were used according to the contemporary report *Soviet Women in the War*, "least frequently of all in actual armed combat." Mainly they served on the industrial-agricultural front.

Russian women were never equal to men politically. After World War II, when there was the greatest shortage of Soviet men, only 17 percent of the Supreme Soviet were women. Only 5 percent served as People's Commissars, and in the highest councils there were no women at all.

Is it any better now? A recent article from the Soviet publication *Zhurnalist* announced that Soviet women "who

| 159

are expected to do everything from digging ditches to pro-
ducing babies are grumbling these days about job discrimination, male chauvinism and lack of concern by Soviet
Authorities." Here, more than fifty years after the revolution
that was supposed to legislate equality, there is a growing
"women's question" in the Soviet Union.

An anonymous Soviet demographer is quoted as asking,
"Why has the idea of real emancipation of women still
not emerged victorious in the public consciousness of both
men and women?"

One Soviet woman's answer was: "The revolution freed
us so that we can work harder than men." Is this the equality
American women are now beginning to fight for in earnest?
Today's Soviet women, according to the article, complain
about the preference given to men in many fields of work.
As a result the women are considered men's equals in doing
heavy manual work, but men generally refuse to do an equal
share of household chores.

In the Soviet Union, as in America, a woman, whether
she be a scientist, doctor, welder or street sweeper, is still
expected to come home at the end of a day's work and
take over the household chores.

The article makes the point that the jobs, now cited as
typically female in Russia, are considered least attractive.
Among these jobs are paving streets, picking up garbage
and digging holes. Even in teaching, medicine and scientific
work—the jobs held for the most part by women—the
supervisory posts go to men.

Many men, according to the Russian publication, would
like to put women back in the kitchen and restore the old-
fashioned environment, and Lenin be damned! They even

confess that many women share this view. However, when faced with the choice of either a job or a family, the typical Soviet woman will opt for a job or career and forget the family. Some married women compromise by restricting themselves to one child.

As to sharing the work with the men, Zoya A. Yankova, a sociologist working for the Academy of Sciences Institute of Social Research and a specialist on woman's problems says:

Very few men, even those from the proletariat, have considered how much they could lighten the burdens and cares of their wives—or even relieve them of them completely—if they would help in "woman's work." But no. This would be against the rights and dignity of men. He demands that he has his rest and comfort. The household life of the woman is a daily sacrifice of herself as a victim to thousands of petty things. The old right of male supremacy continues to exist in concealed forms.

So much for fifty years of a brave new world.

There are those who say the Soviet Union has betrayed the revolution, the Russians are no better than the Americans. They are both imperialist nations and exploiters of women. If this is so, perhaps we can look to China for signs of a real equality between the sexes.

Dr. Arthur W. Galston, professor of biology at Yale University, recently had a two-hour interview with China's Premier Chou En-lai. During the course of the interview Dr. Galston said that he had noticed that there apparently were still few women serving on government committees.

The Premier conceded that progress had been slow. Referring to one top level scientific board he said, "It's true we still only have three women out of a board membership of twenty-one. But our quota is nine, and we're gradually getting there."

The quota of nine, of course, presupposes that even the ideal situation leaves the board weighted in favor of men.

The Fight to Be a Man

What it all boils down to is that men, whether in the Soviet Union, the United States or China, all fight desperately to maintain their place in society and their masculinity. They see masculinity in terms of their relationship to women first, to their jobs second and finally to the rest of society. Their masculinity is threatened, in any relationship with a woman, if they are asked to take on any of the jobs that our culture has labeled "woman's work."

"Why should I do the housework?" a married friend asked me plaintively the other day, smarting at a recent marital injustice. "Hell, that's not my job. The next thing I know she'll be asking me to wear dresses and use perfume and makeup. God damn it, I'm a man, doesn't she realize that?"

Yet even while he complained I could smell the heady scent of a male cologne, a very hot item in the new line of masculine cosmetics.

My friend's complaint, of course, was based on a deeper hurt than simply being asked to assume the culturally feminine role. It was not indignation, but fear. How sure are any of us of our masculinity? Push us into a woman's role and we rebel, we feel threatened. Good heavens, suppose we find we like it? What then?

Similarities Between Men and Women

The questionnaire we analyzed earlier in the book was offered to a Freudian psychoanalyst and a radical member of Women's Lib. They both, very quickly, gave the same answer. "A woman feels womanly because she has a vagina, a man because he has a penis."

They seemed to me strange bedfellows, and yet both used the same simplistic approach of labeling the difference between the sexes the simple possession of a penis or a vagina. Each, of course, drew different implications from the answer.

But even if we consider only physical differences, these become tremendous. We have seen earlier in the chapter that there are developmental differences, hormonal differences, differences of bone structure, susceptibility to disease, stamina and a host of others.

There are also differences in the way men and women think. We explored some of those differences when we considered how men and women view each other and themselves, but the list of differences is almost endless. Consider any subject and you can come up with a woman's view and a man's view. Women see the world differently than men see it. They have a different time sense, a different color sense and a different set of esthetic values.

In their struggle against male domination, women inevitably have accepted the male-dominated world's conviction that what is male is best. It is too late in the anthropological game to try to pretend that no matter what the differences, women could not do as good a job or better than men in any field, war included, if they set their minds to it. Still, the question remains: In doing a traditionally male job is a woman achieving the fullest expression of her own capacities and attributes?

If the women who went into business did not have to compete with men in a man's world, they could function on their own terms and perhaps the result would be less of the cutthroat dishonest management than is now associated with all business. I don't know. As it is, women in business act like men. It would take a probing psychological study to discover what would happen to a business if women ran it like women. I have a feeling that that particular establishment would be a happier place to work in.

The world might be a happier place too, if women were "into" politics. Traditionally women are not politicians. There are almost no female politicians of any stature in the United States, and on the international scene the only ones who come immediately to mind are Golda Meir and Indira Gandhi. This is incredible when you consider that more than half of the voters, in America at any rate, are women. Is this because women haven't a gift for politicking, or because the male-oriented political machines avoid women candidates?

When a woman candidate like Bella Abzug or Shirley Chisholm in New York does get power, she proves that women can be just as politically aggressive as men. But they are still competing in a field where men have set the rules. How different would politics be if women set the ground rules based on their own approach to life? How different would the history of the world have been if women could always have acted like women, not like men, when they reached high places? Would we, in fact, if women could function politically as women, have many more of them in politics?

The Equal Marriage

Take Rosie and Paul. They are both bright and alert young people, both from well-to-do but not rich families, both with good jobs and good prospects.

"We were married," Rosie said, "in a special ceremony we wrote ourselves. It was just beautiful. Our minister agreed to use our words, and we had the ceremony performed at dawn in the park outside of town. Then we had a big breakfast for all the guests on my folks' back lawn."

"We have an equal marriage," Paul said seriously. "We share the work around the house, and we bank an equal amount from our salaries."

The bride and groom found a third-floor walkup apartment in a private house midway between Rosie's work and Paul's. "We both love to walk, and this way we walk to work and back, and each of us covers the same distance each day . . . in different directions."

Paul frowned. "I'm not so happy about that. I don't like Rosie walking home alone at night. It's not all that nice a neighborhood. I'd like to walk with her, but with the apartment where it is . . ."

"The kids fixed the run-down flat over and did a beautiful job," Rosie's father said proudly. "But I don't understand the way they manage things. All that repair work was too hard for a girl."

"Well, I really did most of the painting," Paul admitted. "Rosie claims she gets exhausted after half an hour. I'm still not sure she wasn't taking advantage of me. We did agree to share . . ."

"We share the cooking," Rosie explained. "But lately I've taken to cleaning up all by myself. Not that Paul doesn't want to help, but he's the original Captain Klutz. We've lost half our dishes already and the sink and counters are a mess. He doesn't mind, but I do."

When the baby came, Rosie gave up her job and joked about it. "Paul couldn't take the idea of being pregnant, so I had to have the baby."

"If populating the world depended on men's giving birth, we'd never make it," Paul grinned. "I wouldn't have the guts, but that old lady of mine sailed through natural childbirth."

"Actually I do most of the work involving the baby," Rosie confessed ruefully a year later. "I'm just better at it, and I like it. Paul takes over the hard physical jobs. It works out that way, and really, it makes better sense."

And so it went, the equality that they both accepted and wanted was achieved through an equality of respect, and equality of love, not through an equal division of labor.

Dividing the Work

Purpose: To force the woman to decide how much her traditional role really means to her.

The woman takes one male doll and calls it HUSBAND. She also takes one female doll and calls it WIFE. The woman will play both HUSBAND and WIFE. Using the following list of household tasks, WIFE assigns HUSBAND the jobs she

really wants him to do. The household tasks:

Preparing dinner
Washing dishes
Preparing the market list
Shopping at the market
Taking out the garbage
Mowing the lawn
Paying the household bills
Buying the children's clothing
Selecting gifts
Buying a new chair for the living room
Supervising home repairs
Sewing
Packing the children's lunchbox
Waxing the floor
Cleaning the oven
Preparing breakfast
Setting the table
Planning a vacation
Balancing the checkbook

What to watch for: How many of the jobs she normally performs does the woman really deeply wish to reassign to her husband?

11

Can Marriage Work?

The Game of Marriage

In the first chapter we took a look at Joe and Ann, the seemingly ideal American couple. They looked very nice together, and Norman Rockwell has enshrined them in every stage of their life through endless *Saturday Evening Post* covers. They are alive and well even today, disguised as Julie and David, Ozzie and Harriet, Roy and Dale, and all the other fantasies of American married life. This is the "Barbie" and "Ken" doll marriage we advertise to our children. And we want it to be our marriage too. We expect that it will be. And then somehow it never comes out just that way.

A short time ago I was up in the mountains with my wife inspecting a projected site for our summer house. I was discussing the slope of the land with the builder, a blunt, good-looking man's-kind-of-man in his early forties with a wife and three children. My wife had wandered off to look at a brook, and I called to her, but she couldn't hear me over the noise of the running water.

"I guess she's lost," I told the builder.

"I should be that lucky," he snapped back, without thinking. "My wife never gets lost."

A few minutes later, when we were all headed back to the car, he took me aside and said uncomfortably, "I didn't really mean that. I really love the old lady."

I assured him that I knew he was joking, but I wondered about that joke. You don't snap out an answer that quickly or feel guilty about it later unless there's more than a grain of truth in what you've said. Yet joking about the wife is a good, solid, respected American game that we all play, one of the many games of marriage.

In our pre-children days my wife and I used to be very friendly with a young couple whose apartment we went to on Sunday mornings because "Don made such beautiful waffles."

Sunday morning was a production. Don would put on a canvas apron and start in. "Karen, where are the eggs?"

"Here, dear."

"Karen, get me the flour. Where's the measuring cup? I need two cups of milk! Will you get the baking soda and the buttermilk! Where's the waffle iron, Karen?"

She would scamper dutifully around the kitchen while he mixed the waffle batter and baked the waffles, leaving behind a shambles of pots and food. When it was all over, Karen would look at him adoringly and say, "Don has such a wonderfully light touch with waffles!" And Don would beam modestly.

Three children and fifteen years later and they faced one of the most bitter and violent divorces I've ever heard of.

What had changed? Nothing really. They had simply gotten to the point where the role-playing of the early marriage was meaningless.

Role-playing often works in the early years of a marriage. Karen is delighted to bolster Don's ego, to scurry around the kitchen fetching every ingredient as he orders it. It makes him easier to live with.

In later years she just becomes "fed up with feeding his ego. To hell with that. If you want the goddamn eggs, go to the refrigerator yourself. If you want me to make the waffles, OK. Don't put on such an act."

After the divorce Karen said, "Christ, I'm a human being too. What about my ego?"

And Don muttered, "She's become a ballbreaker. She cuts me down every time I try to do something. Who needs that kind of marriage?"

The second time around, after the divorce, Don married a very sweet, very feminine woman. But was she so sweet or was she still a novice and new at the game, still playing her role?

The Second-Marriage Syndrome

There is a second-marriage syndrome in our society. The case history of the syndrome is very much like Don and Karen's story. I know of another couple in San Francisco, Ralph and Gerda, married twenty-three years and with two grown children. I called them a few months ago when I was in the city, and Gerda answered the phone.

Instant tears. "Did you hear what that bastard did? After twenty-three years he demanded a divorce. Said I emasculated him. Jesus Christ, I was what he wanted. I waited on him hand and foot. I even told him what clothes to wear, and I raised his kids. Is that emasculating?"

And Ralph? He had already remarried. I had drinks at the Top of the Mark with Ralph and his second wife, Eunice. Eunice is short and feminine and very much in love with Ralph. "I had it with Gerda," Ralph confided. "Twenty-three years of being cut down to size! Thank God I had the sense to end it!"

Another case in point is Betty Friedan, the mother of Women's Liberation, and her husband Carl Friedan. After twenty years of marriage they were divorced. Carl married Noreen, a "blond model." His divorce and subsequent remarriage were smeared over most newspapers, and in an interview with Myra Macpherson for the *New York Post*, Carl Friedan said, "I'm delighted with my wife Noreen. She's charming and lovely. She makes chicken soup, and that's love. She shines my shoes sometimes. My image of a wife is certainly not one who never cooks, never stays home. Betty never washed a hundred dishes during twenty years of marriage. That doesn't mean Noreen's some namby-pamby, but she's no intellectual, thank God."

We all encourage our wives to express themselves, but we don't really mean it in its fullest sense. Few men today want intellectual wives or independent wives, or wives who assume the dominant role in managing or earning the family finances. As Lederer concluded in *The Fear of Women:*

As to the man, what he most wants of woman is that she should make him feel most like a man. This is a big demand and no woman can fill it all the time. In marriage, dissatisfactions are built in. No wife can ever be maternal, sexual and intellectual in just the right proportions to suit her husband's needs.

But it goes even deeper than that. Few wives accept the fact early in marriage that they cannot meet their husband's needs. Nor does the woman in the beginning of a marriage consider her own needs. Why should she? The culture in which she spends her adult years is a male-dominated one. The woman who enters marriage is taught that she should love, honor and obey. Only in the last few generations, in more progressive parts of the nation, has the "obey" been dropped.

She comes into marriage fully convinced that she will be happy "serving" her husband, though it is never voiced in this brutal way. The bride may say, "I want to be a real wife. I want to clean and cook, take care of the children and fulfill myself as a woman."

And except for the brief recent flak from Women's Lib, this is what brides are advised to do. This is what they grow up expecting to do, hoping to do.

The Shared Marriage

Here and there we read of different types of marriage. But they are in the great minority. I recently spoke to a young woman who is an ex-member of a western commune where a new type of marriage was attempted. The men and women living there had rejected our society and our values. They had rejected the entire establishment and with it, marriage as we know it. And they tried to live within the framework of a shared marriage.

"But it wasn't right," my young friend moodily said. "It wasn't right for me. Sure we ate organic food and brown rice and soy bean substitutes for meat, but we women were the ones who prepared the meals. We cleaned and kept house. The only difference between that and an old-fashioned marriage is that when we complained that the men were acting like slobs, we were told we still had establishment values.

"And as for sex, it wasn't sharing for the women. We were being used. The men shared us. It was as simple as that."

It is not an uncommon complaint. Many disillusioned young people are already rejecting the new style of shared marriage. Whether or not they will return to simple monogamy remains to be seen. The point is that the communal marriage still caters to man's predatory nature, his need to use women, even when he shares them. And he shares them usually because he has contempt for them. Like any other possession women are his to share or to keep to himself.

Compatibility Through Incompatibility

There has never been any clear-cut resolution to the question, Is man monogamous or polygamous. There have been many claims, mostly by men, that polygamy is a more normal condition and that no man can be expected to be completely faithful. Perhaps this is true. Certainly fidelity is often a difficult state, even when a man deeply loves his wife and children. There is a need in most men to experiment, to reassure themselves that they are still in the running.

Women are thought to have less of this need, though infidelity in a marriage is not the man's province alone. For the most part, however, women seem content with the traditional marital situation. The majority of divorces are initiated by the man, or if the woman starts it, it's because the man has been unfaithful.

Women are usually able to live with the incompatibility of the average marriage. It was Don, not Karen, who asked for the divorce. But of course women have a harder time after divorce. If it were as easy for them to remarry as it is for men, then the divorce rate might soar even higher.

The problem, in any case, centers on our concept of what a male-female relationship should be like, and how we handle that concept. Men and women in our society still enter a relationship expecting to find instant preordained compatibility. What they find instead is instant disappointment.

I think we could make life a great deal easier, a great deal more interesting, and much more romantic for both ourselves and our children if we could give up our storybook models of hero and heroine. Our concept of ideal love is really only a childish fantasy not big enough to encompass true grown-up feelings. Our children watch our marriages fail and question the propaganda we put out. Yet we persist in telling them that there is still such a thing as a perfect match, a match made in heaven.

Why don't we just admit to the truth? What we must learn to do is stop pretending, and start living within the framework of our incompatibility. We must learn not to hate ourselves because we don't live up to our own obsolete ideals.

If we could only accept our differences we would be free to express our honest emotions. The games in this book are designed to turn the stale role-playing of men and women inside out so that they can start communicating across the incompatibility gap. It is only a beginning, and I hope that any couple who finds the games stimulating and helpful will go on to design more games of their own.

Incompatibility, then, can become the key to compatibility. Even as men and women fit together sexually, they also fit together on a non-sexual level. Their very incompatibility, the very differences between the sexes, is the source of their attraction in the first place. If we can learn to stop using our differences as weapons, I think we will find that they can become the building blocks of a new relationship which is at once more realistic, more lasting and more exciting.

Building Blocks

Purpose: This is a reconciliation game.

In this game the man and woman try to remember each other's positive qualities. The game should go on long enough to force each partner to dig deeply to recall assets he may be taking for granted.

The man takes a male doll and gives it his name. The woman takes a female doll and gives it her name. Alternating in rapid succession, each doll must acknowledge a good quality of the other. For example:

He: You've got the prettiest legs I've ever seen on a woman.

She: I like your beard.

He: You're a fantastic cook.

She: You've got a great sense of humor. And so on.

Selected References

Ardrey, R., *The Territorial Imperative*. New York: Atheneum, 1966.

Bird, C., *Born Female*. New York: David McKay, 1968.

Briffault, R., *The Mothers*. New York: Grosset & Dunlap, 1963.

Brook, P., Filming a Masterpiece. *Observer Weekend Review*. July 26, 1964.

Chapman, J. D., *The Feminine Mind and Body*. New York: Philosophical Library, 1967.

de Beauvoir, S., *The Second Sex*. New York: Alfred A. Knopf, Inc., 1953.

Dubos, R., *So Human an Animal*. New York: Scribner's, 1968.

Elwin, V., The Vagina Dentata Legend. *British Journal of Medical Psychology*. 19:439, 1941.

Fast, J., *Body Language*. New York: M. Evans and Co., Inc., 1970.

Ferguson, C. W., *The Male Attitude*. Boston: Little, Brown, 1966.

Figes, E., *Patriarchal Attitudes*. London: Faber & Faber, 1970.

Flexner, E., *Century of Struggle*. Cambridge, Mass.: Belknap Press of Harvard, 1959.

Selected References

FREUD, S., Female Sexuality. *International Journal of Psychoanalysis 13, 1932.*

———. Femininity. *New Introductory Lectures on Psychoanalysis.* New York: Norton, 1965

FRIEDAN, B., *The Feminine Mystique.* New York: Norton, 1963.

GOLDING, W., *Lord of the Flies.* New York: Coward-McCann, 1968.

GREER, G., *The Female Eunuch.* New York: McGraw-Hill, 1971.

HALL, E. T., *The Hidden Dimension.* Garden City, N.Y.: Anchor Books, Doubleday, 1969.

HORNEY, K., The Dread of Women. *International Journal Psychoanalysis.* 13:348, 1932.

———. The Flight from Womanhood: The Masculinity-Complex in Women. *International Journal Psychoanalysis,* Vol. 7. Oct., 1926.

JEANNIERE, A., *The Anthropology of Sex.* New York: Harper, 1967.

KANOWITZ, L., *Women and the Law.* Albuquerque: University of New Mexico Press, 1969.

KAUFMAN, S., *Diary of a Mad Housewife.* New York: Random House, 1967.

KINSEY, A., *Sexual Behavior in the Human Female.* Philadelphia: Saunders, 1953.

KIRKENDALL, L. A. (ed.), *The New Sexual Revolution.* New York: Donald W. Brown, 1971.

KUYNETS, G. M. & Q. McNEMAR, Sex Differences in Intelligence Test Scores, in Intelligence; Its Nature and Nurture. 1940 *Yearbook. Natl. Soc. for Study of Educ.* *39* (1):211.

LEDERER, W., *The Fear of Women.* New York: Harcourt Brace Jovanovich, 1968.

LORENZ, K., *On Aggression.* New York: Harcourt Brace Jovanovich, 1966.

MAILER, N., *An American Dream.* New York: Dial Press, 1964.

——. The Prisoner of Sex. *Harper's Magazine,* March 1971.

MALINOWSKI, B., *The Sexual Life of Savages.* New York: Harcourt Brace Jovanovich, 1929.

MASTERS, R. E. L., *The Anti-Sex.* New York: Julian Press, 1964.

MASTERS, W. H., JOHNSON, V. E., *Human Sexual Response.* Boston: Little, Brown, 1966.

MEAD, M., *Culture and Commitment.* New York: Doubleday, 1970.

——. *Male and Female.* New York: Dell, 1968.

MEMMI, A., *Dominated Man.* New York: Orion Press, 1968.

MILLER, H., *Tropic of Capricorn.* New York: Grove Press, 1961.

——. *Sexus.* New York: Grove Press, 1962.

MILLETT, K., *Sexual Politics.* New York: Doubleday, 1970.

MISHIMA, Y., *Kinjiki.* Published in America as *Forbidden Colors.* New York: Alfred A. Knopf, 1968.

Selected References

MONTAGU, A., *The Natural Superiority of Women*. New York: Macmillan, 1968.

———. (ed.) *Culture and the Evolution of Man*. New York: Oxford University Press, 1962.

MORGAN, R., (ed.) *Sisterhood Is Powerful*. New York: Vintage Books, 1970.

MORRIS, D., *The Naked Ape*. New York: McGraw-Hill, 1967.

ORTEGA Y GASSET, J., *Man and People*. New York: Norton, 1961.

———. *On Love: Aspects of a Single Theme*. New York: Meridian, 1957.

PARTURIER, F., *Open Letter to Men*. London: Heinemann, 1968.

REICHARD, S. & C. TILLMAN, Patterns of Parent-Child Relationships in Schizophrenia. *Psychiatry*, 13:247–257, 1950.

REIK, T., *Of Love and Lust*. New York: Farrar, Straus & Giroux, 1941.

ROSZAK, B. AND T., *Masculine/Feminine*. New York: Harper & Row, 1969.

RUITENBECK, H. M., *Sexuality and Identity*. New York: Dell, 1970.

SCHEINFELD, A., *Women and Men*. New York: Harcourt Brace Jovanovich, 1943.

SCHOFIELD, M., *The Sexual Behavior of Young People*. Boston: Little, Brown, 1965.

SCOTT-MAXWELL, *Women and Sometimes Men*. New York: Alfred A. Knopf, 1957.

SHAW, G. B., *Getting Married* (in) *Edwardian Plays.* Gerald Weales, ed. Hill and Wang, 1962.

SINCLAIR, A., *The Emancipation of the American Woman.* New York: Harper & Row, 1966.

Soviet Women in the War, *Bull. American Russian Institute,* No. 27, March 31, 1942.

SPITZ, RENÉ A., The Psychogenic Diseases of Infancy. Psychoanalytic Study of the Child, Vol. VI, 1951. New York: International Universities Press, 1951.

STERN, K., *The Flight from Women.* New York: Farrar, Straus & Giroux, 1965.

STOLLER, R. J., *Sex and Gender.* New York: Science House, 1968.

TERMAN, L. M. et al., Genetic Studies of Genius, Vol. III, 1930.

TIGER, L., *Men in Groups.* New York: Vintage Books, 1970.

WATTS, A., *Nature, Man and Woman.* New York: Pantheon, 1958.

WILSON, C., Promiscuity and the Casanova Impulse (in) *The Origin of Sexual Impulse.* New York: Putnam's, 1963.

WYLIE, P., *Generation of Vipers.* New York: Rinehart & Co., 1955 (1942).

YOUNG, W. C., (ed.) Sex and Internal Secretions, Vol. 2. Baltimore: Williams and Wilkins, 1961.

To Make the Dolls:

Trace the outlines on the following pages onto tracing or tissue paper (or onto thin typing paper if you can see through it). Cut out your tracing and you will have the basic outline of the doll. If you use tracing or tissue paper and would like to have a sturdier doll to use in the games, cut out your tracing, draw around it onto heavier paper, cut it—and you will have a sturdy doll. In this way you can make as many dolls as you need for any particular game.

N

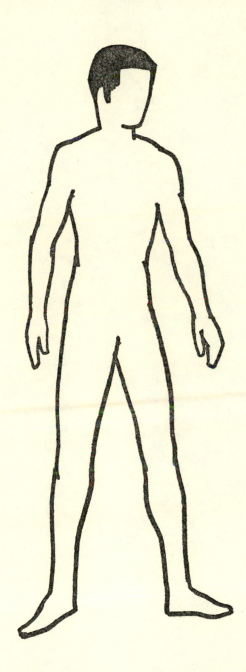

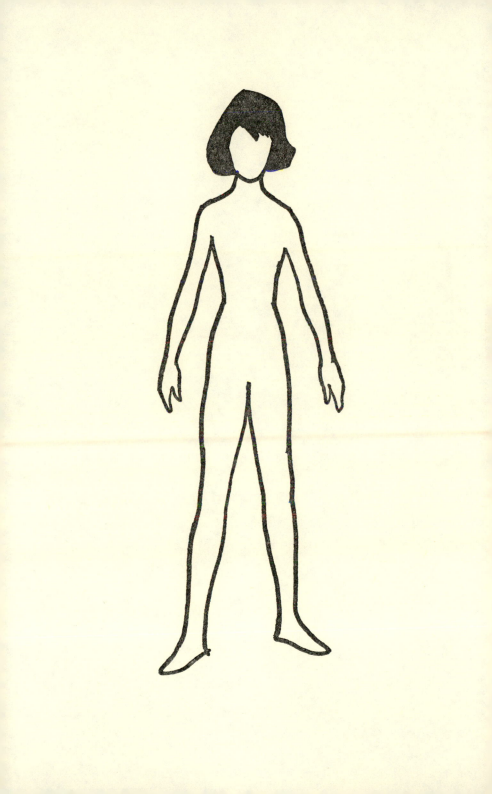